Teaching with Influence

Teaching with Influence

PETER HOOK AND ANDY VASS

David Fulton Publishers
London

David Fulton Publishers
2 Park Square, Milton Park, Abingdon, Oxon OX14 4RN

270 Madison Avenue, New York, NY 10016

First published in Great Britain in 2002 by David Fulton Publishers
Transferred to digital printing

David Fulton Publishers is an imprint of the Taylor & Francis Group, an informa business

British Library Cataloguing in Publication Data
A catalogue record for this book is available from the British Library.

ISBN 1-85346-692-1

Typeset by Servis Filmsetting Ltd, Manchester

Contents

About us . . .

Peter Hook and Andy Vass are two of the foremost motivational trainers in the UK, and through their unique company – Gillmans Consultancy – they have created a portfolio of proven success, specialising in:

- Social inclusion
- Positive behaviour management
- Individual and organisational coaching
- Team development and motivation
- Emotional intelligence
- Brain-based learning
- Student motivation

They can be contacted by email at: info@gillmans.biz

Alternatively, you can write to them at:

Gillmans Consultancy
24 Kings Road
Tonbridge
Kent
TN9 2HD
United Kingdom

Acknowledgements

We would like to thank

- Our wives for sharing the knowledge and understanding derived from being emotionally inspirational teachers.
- Our children for their experiences of being taught and their insights into what makes a difference in classrooms.
- The many teachers we have worked with in schools and workshops. Their feedback has been encouraging and has provided invaluable support.
- All the students we have worked with for confirming that what we believe in and what is contained here makes a difference.

The ideas and information here are the result of a long teaching career and an eclectic mix of working with some outstanding teachers, learning from our own experiences and reading avidly. We are always keen to acknowledge the influences on our work but if any have been omitted, it is not deliberate on our part. If you recognise something that we haven't credited you with, please let us know and we will make amends in the next book.

How to get the most from this book

- Make the information here relevant to you. There is a wide margin for writing ideas, jotting key words or noting some personal responses to questions posed both within the text and in the activity sheets.
- At the end of the chapter there are 'Questions for professional development.' These may be used as part of your professional development portfolio.

Start by getting the big picture

- Scan through the book stopping wherever you get the urge to do so. Look at the contents page and the key point summaries. Do whatever it takes for you to get a feel for what the book can do for you.
- Begin to make connections between the ideas, strategies and skills contained in the book and aspects of your own experience. How will what is on offer here support you in your classroom? In what ways does it match or connect with what you know already? What ideas are unusual or different to how you behave in class?

Formulate your own goals

- What is it *specifically* you want to know from this book? What would you need to know to become even better at what you do?
- What kind of things would you like to be able to do as you become increasingly influential?

Give us feedback

We are genuinely keen to receive *any* feedback and will make every effort to include them in newsletters, subsequent editions or other books:

- further questions you may have
- experiences of implementing the strategies
- any successful ideas or variations you have discovered
- ideas that haven't worked – yet!

You will find a contact email above – we always reply.

Introduction

An ongoing journey

Learning is a full-blooded, human, social process, and so is teaching.
R.W. Connell, *Schools and Social Justice*

Welcome to this, our third, book on the journey towards becoming the sort of teacher you would aspire to be. This book invites you to consider the influential nature of your work with young people.

Throughout their careers, teachers touch the lives of thousands of young people; without their commitment and participation, attempts to improve the school system are bound to fail.
For the Love of Learning: The Bégin-Caplan Report 1995

Influencing students is not an option. Simply by being a teacher, you will influence the lives of all of the students you encounter and this influence may be for good or bad – the choice is yours.

You will undoubtedly have already been a significant, positive influence upon the lives of students. This influence may not always be immediately visible; it may be masked, at the moment, by other factors that overwhelm the lives of some of our students but, nevertheless, your influence will be present.

As we have invited you to do in previous books, again we invite you to begin this book by thinking now of people who created that small (or major) therapeutic force in your life. In particular, who were your favourite teachers, the ones who influenced and inspired you and made you feel important, the ones who had confidence in you, who made the time to listen and valued what you said? As you think of those people, what was it about them that can still create these emotions in you? Of course, they had a style and manner of working with their students and, obviously, the things they said and the way they said them made a big difference.

What we're asking you to consider now is:

What beliefs did they hold that allowed them to be this way?

What were the values that directed their behaviour?

How were they able to create for themselves the physical state and intellectual frame of mind to persistently and unconditionally create that spark in you and many others?

What part of them did they allow you access to?

Our belief is that these people you have been thinking about had one thing in common: they believed with a passion that what they were doing was right; they had a vision of how they wanted the emotional, intellectual and physical climate of their classrooms to be; they articulated and lived those beliefs and visions – they 'walked the talk'. They also had realistic beliefs about what teachers do; they appreciated the personal qualities they possessed; they understood how these supported and encouraged them in their classroom leadership. Most of all, they passionately cared about how to help their students become 'winners'.

Teaching with Influence is the third of a trilogy of books that began with *Confident Classroom Leadership* and moved on through *Creating Winning Classrooms*. We have designed it to build upon the skills and concepts outlined in these two previous books and we therefore hope that you will find within these covers the same style of practical ideas and user-friendly concepts that will enable you to continue to refine your skills both within and beyond the classroom. This book will provide you with reassurance and confidence that there are solutions to what may seem frustrating and emotionally fraught situations, and reassurance that it takes time, effort and strength of belief to become a truly influential teacher.

Influential teachers acquire, develop and refine their skills during the process of gaining experience. Seeing how your confidence will grow, how you will sound more relaxed and feel more in control, comes from being presented with a wide range of alternative practical strategies that *really* work in a format that allows you to integrate them comfortably into your existing practice.

Take responsibility

For what, in the context of your classroom, are you responsible? Is responsibility the same as control? If there are things happening in your classrooms that you do not like and you do not take responsibility for managing them, you won't be able to change them. It is always easier to find reasons why we can't do something. Beware of giving mental space to problem-centred thinking that attributes causation and blame on parenting skills, the home environment, scarce resources, school management, the National Curriculum, government policy, Ofsted, etc. While we can't control how Nathan spends his time in the evenings, or the fact that he comes from a violent and dysfunctional family and arrives in school tired and very hungry, we can take responsibility for how *we* respond to this baggage and how we manage his behaviour. Pay attention to what you can do something about. That's what we mean by taking responsibility. If what you try doesn't work, do it differently. That's also what we mean by responsibility.

To bring about change you have to actually do something that is different. To move along your journey to the kind of classroom you want, to becoming the kind of teacher you wish to be requires that you do something to make it happen. Often this will mean taking a risk, leaving your comfort zone and, on many occasions, getting it wrong. Students do not expect teachers to be perfect. They expect them to be human, to be fallible and to be able to deal with it honestly and with humility.

There are a number of skills that are common to highly effective teachers. In this book you will certainly gain an insight into those skills but, more than that, you will have access to the beliefs that effective teachers hold about themselves and their students; not only what effective teachers do but also *how* they manage to do it.

Take action

If, as you use this book, you spend time noticing what we haven't included, you'll be right. You will also be wasting precious energy. If you think about the times when some of the skills wouldn't work, you'll be right again.

If, however, as you read this book we engage you in thinking about things you'd like to be able to do, we recommend you devote energy and time to learning how to do them.

Keep an open mind

Chapter 1

Influence-v-Coercion

A teacher affects eternity; he can never tell where his influence stops.
Henry Adams, *The Education of Henry Adams*

*Being a teacher is not just a matter of having a body of knowledge and
a capacity to control a classroom. That could be done by a computer with
a cattle prod. Just as important, being a teacher means being able to
establish human relations with the people being taught.*
The Bégin-Caplan Report 1995

Commit this to memory:

> **IT IS NOT POSSIBLE TO CONTROL STUDENT BEHAVIOUR
> IN YOUR CLASSROOM**

In a staffroom a few weeks ago the bell began to ring for the
start of Period 2. Some teachers had already set off and others
were, rather more reluctantly, downing the last sips of tea
and stirring from their chairs. A few teachers were already
setting the scene for what was to come: *'OK. Let's go and show
them who's boss.' 'I hope that little **** Kyle isn't in again, he
makes me so mad.' 'Let's see how many pearls disappear down the
throats of the swine this time.' 'Don't shoot till you see the whites
of their eyes.'* Some of these teachers are emotionally burned
out; some have just become cynical; others have come to see
the students as the emotional 'enemy'. All of them have
developed the 'us against them' attitude that has its roots in
the false belief that it is possible to control student behaviour.

Of all the things in your classroom over which you have some element
of control, the behaviour of others is *not* one of them. This is the
demanding reality that you forget at your peril. This simple yet, for
many teachers, challenging truth is your key to becoming one of that
highly successful group of teachers who are genuinely influential in
their dealings with students.

Nevertheless, this simple truth is something that far too many teachers never come to understand and accept. They go through their teaching careers believing that the control of student behaviour is possible. They expend vast amounts of physical and, more importantly, psychological and emotional energy on the only part of the behavioural dynamic over which they have absolutely no control.

Some teachers are so firmly convinced that they can control student behaviour that, when faced with the evidence that their controlling efforts are coming to nothing, instead of searching for a better approach, they become even more controlling in their actions, thoughts and intents. They create even more rules in their classrooms and enforce them with increasing rigour. They set up increasing numbers of regulations and procedures. They use more and more severe punishments. The balance between rewards and sanctions (the sanctions always being skewed in favour of punishment with these teachers) begins to tip even more away from rewards. The worst of them begin to resort to sarcasm, insults and humiliation to try and cow the students into submission. They become the living embodiment of the old – and extremely counterproductive – adage *'Don't smile until Christmas.'* Only, for them, Christmas is far too soon! Their stress levels show a markedly upward turn. And still their students show no sign of bowing under this pressure. In fact, some of their students are now starting to actively rebel against this increasingly repressive, authoritarian regime.

These teachers then make their last and, sometimes, fatal mistake – they start to develop explanatory models both for their lack of success in exercising control and their increasing levels of stress. *'It's them – they're mad.' 'The class is mad.' 'What can you do with them? Look where they grew up.' 'You only have to meet her mum to see where the problem is.' 'His parents can't even be bothered to teach him good manners.'* Some of these may indeed be part of the setting factors within which students make choices about their behaviour, but as these teachers begin more and more to see these factors as *characteristics* of the students, they cease to be explanatory models and become excuses. These teachers start to feel even more disempowered. They may begin to send more and more students out of their lessons to the Senior Management Team to be 'dealt with'. When these students return to their classrooms, unharmed and unchanged, they start to blame others for their increasingly stressful situation: *'The Headteacher isn't supportive', 'It's alright for them, they don't understand what it's like day in, day out.'* Once this blaming becomes entrenched these teachers are very difficult to help and support. They have established a thick brick wall that says, *'It's not me it's them, so why should I change?'* Many of these teachers will become ill; some will have to leave the profession early; some will have heart attacks.

Essentially this style of classroom management has the following features:

- A reactive stance – these teachers do not plan interactions, they react to circumstances;

- A blaming culture – these teachers hold the students responsible for causing the negative feelings that they experience;
- The teacher as victim – they see themselves as the victim of other people's decisions and actions;
- 'Us and them' – these teachers do not see themselves as part of the classroom dynamic. Rather, they see themselves as external agents trying to control the uncontrollable;
- Win/lose interactions – these teachers win at the expense of the students. Power is everything and is centred (so these teachers believe) within the teacher.

In an era when teachers are under increasing external pressure to constantly improve results, achieve externally imposed targets and provide data to support their work, it makes sense to adopt as many stress-reducing strategies and beliefs as possible. Putting a lot of emotional and physical energy into trying to achieve the impossible not only makes no sense – it can become professional suicide.

Classrooms are infinitely complex systems – take 8Y as an example.

> 8Y are by no means the 'class from hell'. They are what could be described – if ever one could be – as an average class. On a good day they can be a joy to teach. On a more difficult day they can be 'challenging but manageable'. The students in 8Y bring to their lessons a constantly changing mix of emotions and social agendas. The range of both physical and emotional maturity within the group is extraordinary. They are all at varying and sometimes conflicting points in their own physical, social and emotional development. They come from a mix of backgrounds that can either support or contradict your best efforts. One of them brings in the heavy emotional baggage of abuse and maltreatment. Their friendship patterns are constantly shifting, breaking and reforming. They are all learning and trying out new social as well as academic skills. Into this already intricate mix is thrown the complexity of a range of preferred learning styles, the effects of diet – many arrive without breakfast and then graze on a diet of e-numbers and fizzy drinks – and the constraints and demands of an increasingly prescriptive curriculum, to name just a few!

If you were one of 8Y's teachers – and many of you will have your own version of '8Y' in mind – to believe that it is possible for you to directly and simultaneously control this entire, ever-changing kaleidoscope of physical, social and emotional development and interchange would be ludicrous in the extreme.

Do not fall for the seductive Siren calling you to try and directly control student behaviour.

Does this mean that you have no control whatsoever in the classroom? Of course it doesn't. You have a great deal of control. Its focus just isn't upon controlling student behaviour.

We are sure that almost all of you will have come across the 'ABC' of behaviour management:

A = Antecedents

This refers to the context in which the behaviour occurs or what is happening in the environment at the time the behaviour occurs. These factors can be many and varied. They can range from the students home circumstances, through their prior learning experiences to what they had (or didn't have) for breakfast or which teacher they had for the previous lesson.

B = Behaviour

This refers to the *actual* behaviour that the student (or teacher) exhibits. Behaviourist approaches lay much emphasis upon the description of what is actually seen – 'Talking to another student after I asked her not to' – rather than allowing excursions into explanatory fictions or over-interpretations – 'Deliberately defying my instructions'. Wheldall and Merrett (1989) describe this approach as 'pinpointing' behaviour.

C = Consequences

This refers to those things that happen after the student has displayed the behaviour. In behaviourist terms the most significant consequences are frequently described as positive and negative reinforcers. In other words, they are those actions or events that either encourage the behaviour to be repeated or are likely to deter the behaviour in the future.

The ABC approach is firmly rooted within the behaviourist school of understanding and stems from researchers such as Pavlov. While it can be useful in helping us begin to explain the sequence associated with some of the behaviours we see in classrooms, we believe it can lead to a very 'sticking plaster' approach to providing support to students and should not be used as a sole method of identifying supportive strategies. The ABC model provides us with a useful metaphor to identify the variety of ways in which you can become even more effective in the classroom because, to a greater or lesser extent, you have some element of control over the A and C parts of the behavioural equation.

You can manage some, but not all, of the antecedents. You can decide where and how you display student work, where you stand to greet students, how you initiate conversations, utilise seating plans and establish entry routines, etc. You have virtually no control over other antecedents such as poor housing, lack of appropriate parenting skills, etc.

Your prime focus for expending your physical and emotional energy should be on identifying strategies for managing and, whenever possible, controlling the C part of the equation. In particular, the only element over which you have total and absolute control in your classroom is *how you choose to emotionally respond to student behaviour*.

This is where we need to introduce you to another, but substantially more influential, set of letters:

$$E + R = O$$

This is not mathematics. It is the basic formula for personal empowerment and proactivity. It represents the key to both your success in the classroom (or the whole of your life if you choose to use it in all aspects of your interactions with others) and in providing effective support to students in their social and emotional development. Translated, it means:

The Events in your life added to your Response give you your Outcomes.

You can choose how you respond to the events in your life. Effective teachers focus their energies on the only thing over which they have direct control – their own behaviour. In this way they become more and more *influential* in their classroom. This is one of the essential keys to becoming even more effective in your classroom. Realise that while you cannot control the behaviour of your students, you can become highly influential.

> *I have come to a frightening conclusion. I am the decisive element in the classroom. It is my personal approach that creates the climate. It is my daily mood that makes the weather. As a teacher I possess tremendous power to make a child's life miserable or joyous. I can be a tool of torture or an instrument of inspiration. I can humble or humour, hurt or heal. In all sets it is my response that decides whether a crisis will be exacerbated or de-escalated – a child humanised or dehumanised.*
> Ginott (1972)

> Wayne and Shaqib are chatting away to each other after you have given the specific direction for independent seatwork – *'No talking for ten minutes. If you have anything to say, put up your hands.'*
> You have a choice . . .
> You could choose to go over and say, *'I'm sick of you two! Every time I ask you to get on with your work, you deliberately defy me! If you can't be bothered to get on with your work, why should I be bothered to teach you? I'll see you both at lunch-time and you can have a detention after school on Thursday. Get on with your work, now!'*
> Or, you could choose to say something like, *'Wayne and*

Shaqib. The direction was for independent seatwork. If you choose not to do that then you will be choosing to talk to me at lunch. Remember, if you want to say anything, put up your hands. Back on task now, thanks.'

The choice is yours and we'll leave you to make up your mind about which choice is likely to achieve the better long-term result.

Highly effective teachers have a model of control that begins within them. They learn to control their own behaviour and, in particular, they realise that their greatest influence will come when they take control of their own emotional responses to students. Nobody makes them do or feel anything – they *choose* their response. This is your key to professional and personal empowerment.

Their classrooms are characterised by:

- A proactive stance – these teachers plan interactions, they make conscious choices about their response to circumstances;
- A 'response-able' culture – these teachers realise that students do not make them feel or do anything. The realisation that both students and teachers choose their response is central to all aspects of interpersonal transactions;
- The teacher leader – they see themselves as the ones responsible for setting the emotional climate in the classroom;
- 'We' – these teachers see themselves as a key part of the classroom dynamic. They realise that by managing their responses they can become increasingly influential;
- Win/win interactions – these teachers consistently seek to create situations in which both the students and they can get their needs met.

Dr Stephen Covey in his highly influential book *The 7 Habits of Highly Effective People* discusses the notion of circles of influence and circles of concern (Figure 1.1). We have found this is such a useful concept that we will briefly share our version of it with you here.

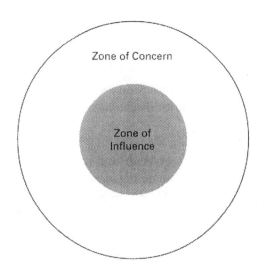

Figure 1.1

There are many things that concern or affect you in both your private and professional life: the National Curriculum, the nuclear energy debate, the timetable, your family, taxes, your classroom seating plan, the balance you put between encouragement and correction. Some of these you can do nothing about and others are directly within your control.

Those that you can do little or nothing about are located within your Zone of Concern. Those over which you can exercise a certain degree of proactivity are placed in your Zone of Influence.

You might like to try Exercise 1 at the end of this chapter before reading on.

By looking at where we spend most of our time and emotional energy we can easily gain a measure of how proactive – and therefore influential – we are. Proactive people focus most of their energy within their Zone of Influence. They focus on the things that they can do something about. Their emotional energy and time has a positive focus. They adopt an 'I can' attitude to the issues that surround them. Their own actions not only empower others, they empower themselves. Success breeds success. Gradually, as they become more proactive and influential, they find that their Zone of Influence expands and things that, only a short time ago, were in their Zone of Concern gradually come into their Zone of Influence (Figure 1.2).

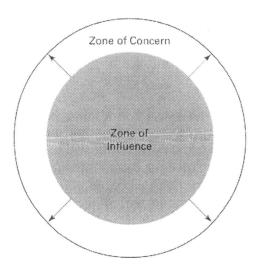

Figure 1.2

Reactive, disempowered teachers focus their efforts upon their Zone of Concern. They focus upon the weaknesses of students and other teachers, the difficulties in the organisation structure and a whole host of other things over which they have little or no influence. They generate negative emotional energy by focusing upon those issues over which they have no control. They not only disempower themselves, they disempower others by their increasingly negative and controlling approach. Gradually and surely, their Zone of Influence diminishes (Figure 1.3).

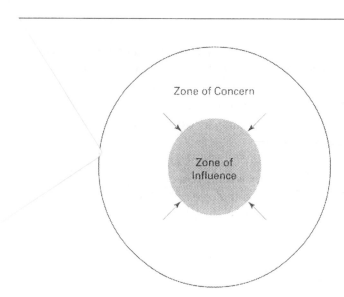

Zone of Concern

Zone of
Influence

Figure 1.3

The remainder of this book will focus upon ways in which, by continually developing your strategies and understandings, you can increasingly become more proactive and influential and turn your focus upon those features that are within your Zone of Influence and minimise those aspects that lie within your Zone of Concern. However, we would like to share one further model that can help us to understand the influential balance between rewards and sanctions, the true role of sanctions and where some teachers make yet another serious mistake in their relationships with students. This model is derived from simple dog training strategies.

The 'dog training' model for the influential use of praise and reprimand

When you first begin the process of training a young puppy to walk to heel on a lead, the process is both simple and effective. You buy a large linked 'choke' type lead and, while walking with the puppy, you briefly tug on the lead, give the command 'Heel' and then praise the puppy immediately. You don't withhold your praise until the puppy is fully trained and walking to heel off the lead. You praise when the puppy shows the first possibility of an inclination of compliance. Nor do you praise once only. The simple strategy is: Limit – Praise – Praise – Praise. Gradually, over time you have to apply less and less and softer and softer limits but the amount of praise remains the same or, frequently, increases.

These are the same procedures adopted by highly influential teachers. Their sanctions or negative consequences are simply limiters – they are the firm tugs on the lead. They then praise students when they show the first signs of compliance. They don't wait until the students are sitting at their desks saying 'Teach me, please' before they praise them! Nor do they only praise them once. The frequency of their praise far outweighs their limiting behaviour.

Ineffective dog trainers simply tug on the lead over and over again. They use the strategy of 'Limit – Limit – Limit'. We are sure that you are all too aware of the effect this has on the puppy. The puppy learns just how hard to pull back on the lead and will continue to do so for the rest of its life. It will take a highly skilled dog trainer to overcome this behaviour and bring the dog back. So it is with teachers who simply apply negative consequence after negative consequence. Students learn just how far to push the boundaries with this teacher. Some of the more exuberant ones will apply considerable psychological pressure on this teacher's 'lead'.

Highly influential teachers realise that their reprimands and negative consequences are best used sparingly and only to describe the limits within the classroom. They recognise that effective reprimands and negative consequences cause unacceptable behaviour to cease for long enough for the teacher to use praise and positive consequences to reinforce the new, more acceptable choice.

Exercise 1

Zones of influence and concern

Get yourself a large sheet of paper and draw two large, concentric circles on it.

Think of an issue that you are currently facing in your classroom. Maybe a whole class. Maybe an individual student.

Begin to list all of the issues involved but, as you do so, decide whether they should fit into your Zone of Influence (you can do something about them) or your Zone of Concern (they affect your work but you have little or no control over them).

Decide which of those factors that are within your Zone of Influence you are going to take control of the next time you are in the classroom (or sooner if that is possible). Make concrete plans. Commit to doing something. Become proactive.

Questions for professional development

What do you feel about the topics covered in this chapter?

What are some of the implications of the topics within your classroom?

What do you think is the most important for you to remember from this chapter?

Chapter 2

The influence of beliefs

One person with a belief is equal to a force of 99 who have only interests.
John Stuart Mill

In this chapter we will explore some highly practical ideas and strategies that will support you in making even more effective choices about your own actions, thoughts and beliefs, which in turn will positively influence the behaviours and thinking of your students.

In Chapter 1 we explained that the only thing you have real control over is your own behaviour. If it is not possible for you (or any other teacher) to control the behaviour of students then the degree of *influence* you are able to exert over different circumstances becomes vitally important. Influence comes in many guises. Effective classroom teachers recognise that on their good days they variously instruct; guide; encourage; persuade; cajole; negotiate; employ consequences; lean heavily on relationships and trust built over time; go temporarily overdrawn on their emotional investments in students (Hook and Vass 2000b) on occasions; and have many other similar interpersonal responses in order to establish and maintain an empowering and supportive classroom climate. The impact and effectiveness of all of the above is that not only is each of them a strategy, which has a bearing in shaping positive outcomes, but also that they are utilised with the intent to protect mutual rights and are in the best interests of the students. In other words, influence is most effective and easier to exert when we approach situations with a win/win attitude.

The obvious question is how do you go about gaining and then using, in a mutually beneficial way, this influence? Moreover, how are you able to actually *increase* the levels of influence available to you in your classroom? What will help you make these changes to your practice?

In a climate of relentless change in which teachers and support staff find themselves, talking about making further changes relating to issues as potentially challenging as managing student behaviour

Making changes

more effectively may, up until now, have been a source of some discomfort. Fortunately, therefore, as you read on and consider our realistic perspective on the nature and process of the changes we refer to throughout the book, you can begin to feel more comfortable exploring some useful changes that bring the possibility of enhancing your ability to teach with increasing influence.

Any changes that you choose to make should be based on the principle that,

> *'If what you are doing isn't working – do something different.'*

However, as this book offers you ideas and strategies in the *'something different'* category, you will become aware that we only talk about very small yet significant differences. Essentially, there are two reasons for this:

1. People, generally, do not make large or wholesale changes in the things they do. Change tends to be incremental.
2. Within your professional life there is no scope for big changes because you are already making a powerful and productive difference in children's lives.

It is far more appropriate to talk about shifts, tweaks, adjustments or refinements when referring to changes in working practice. A further reason that this makes sound sense is to be found in a belief that we have embedded in all our work whether it is working directly with students at risk, coaching and supporting teachers in class, leading workshops or through consultancy in schools.

> It is always more effective to amplify and enhance what is already working than to try to rebuild things from scratch.

In the exercise at the end of Chapter 1 you will have noticed that the majority of the issues that made the difference between a satisfactory and a less pleasing outcome were within your Zone of Influence. They were things that you could do something about and that is highly encouraging. As you engage in the activity below now, be warned that there's a possibility that you will feel even more encouraged!

Consider a scale like a thermometer running from 0 to 10. When you have read the remaining information then award yourself a score on this scale based on *your own* perception of how successfully you positively influence the learning and behavioural outcomes in your classes. Recognise that there are some children and some classes (and some days of the week) where the score will be higher or lower, so go for an average.

NB. On the scale, 0 represents staying in bed with a headache and 10 represents the little voice in your head saying 'I can cope with anything today!'

Look up from this page and award yourself the mark NOW.

Now think of a *specific* time, whether it's a whole lesson, a section of a lesson, a particular activity or even an interaction with a particular student for which, were you only thinking of this, your score would have been higher. Think very carefully and in a detailed way of that specific time so that you are able to recreate it right now and then answer these questions. It often helps to do this with someone, as the answers you give them are likely to be different to the ones you give yourself in your head.

How come your score was higher? What was different about this particular time? What were you thinking differently, feeling differently, saying differently or believing differently to affect a more valuable outcome?

What you have just achieved is the process of articulating (internally or externally) what you do when you are being even more influential than normal. It is very likely that you noticed that some of the factors, which enhanced your influence, were connected to the kind of things you were thinking and the way you felt (physically and emotionally) at the time as well as the things you said and did. How true is it that the things that allowed your score to be higher were, in the main, quite small differences?

> Small changes ARE significant.

The process you have just engaged in is very powerful because it represents an often overlooked aspect in making changes. When you decide that you want to 'tweak' your practice in some way to, for instance, experience an increase in satisfactory interactions, reduce levels of stress and move towards more positive relationships with students, it will be important to answer three questions.

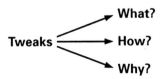

Figure 2.1 Information needed to make small changes

What?

It is important to be very specific about what you are intending to tweak. *'Enhance the quality of working relationships in my classroom'* will not have the desired effect because it is far too global. On the other hand, *'Increase the ratio of praise to correction with Yr 4 or 9G over the next three weeks'* fits well with the notion of SMART (specific, measurable, achievable, realistic and time-framed) targets.

How?

What specific strategies will I use to achieve my intended 'tweak'? What do I already do well or know about this that will help? Is it a question of just doing these things a little more rather than changing anything? Should I target a specific group of students to increase praise to? Is there a friend who could watch for my strategy and give me sensitive feedback?

Why?

At one level, this is about motivation. The 'why' question is closely and legitimately associated with WIIFM (what's in it for me?). If there is no perceivable benefit accruing from the effort of change (however small that effort is), the 'what' and the 'how' become irrelevant. However, the reasons for change crucially need also to encompass a clear cognitive understanding of why this change would not only be valuable but also has a high probability of success. In other words, *why* doing this, saying this or believing this actually works. While knowing what and how to alter things will need to be a deliberate act, which is practised, a conscious understanding of why this is successful is vital. Remembering what we have said above about how powerful amplifying what already works is, understanding why you are as good as you are becomes the key to change.

When you have an understanding of why you are as good as you are in your work, you have three useful possibilities to support change.

1. You can do it more. When you do what works more often, there is less time for things to go wrong.
2. You can share it with colleagues. Not until you can articulate your good practice does it become possible for you to influence your colleagues and pass on your skills.
3. Under the stress and tension involved in teaching, good practice sometimes deserts us. At those times, we are prone to what Daniel Goleman (1996) describes as 'emotional hijacking'. He refers to those times when our responses are more driven by bile and annoyance than reflective good practice. When you know why you're as good as you are, you can hang on to that good practice for longer even under stress and tension.

We first referred to congruence in *Confident Classroom Leadership* (Hook and Vass 2000a) as the ability to match verbal and non-verbal repertoires in communication. All of us have bumped into an acquaintance who claimed they are pleased to see us and yet instinctively we know that they don't *really* mean it. What we are witnessing through our senses is incongruence. It has been said, in describing students, particularly adolescents, that they have highly tuned 'bullshit monitors'. They are able to discern insincerity, lack of conviction, patronising remarks, whether we really like them, as well as hidden messages in our speech with unerring accuracy. They respond to these situations much as adults would do – by withdrawing trust, increasing suspicion and keeping working relationships at arm's length. In fact, exactly the kind of climate that significantly dilutes or even inhibits any possibility of positive influence.

What we are saying is simply this. The reality of working in today's classrooms places significant stresses and strains on our emotional and physical energy. The inevitable product of this is that we say and do things, which are reactionary by nature, uncharacteristically (hopefully) hostile and which we often regret afterwards. Common sense dictates that there will always be occasions such as these and no amount of DfES directives, Ofsted guidelines, behaviour policies or good practice documents will eliminate human fallibility.

If these 'normal but rare' occasions become increasingly frequent then the nature of our influence will be to generate uncertainty in our students, create barriers to learning and distance our students from us. It makes sense therefore to find ways to reduce those occasions to an absolute minimum, to seek out alternatives to the emotional hijacking and to take steps to minimise or dilute the tensions present when it does. By exploring a further element contained in congruent behaviour, we can find some strategies and ideas that help us do just that.

Congruence is easier to attain and only truly genuine when what we say and do emerges from a set of beliefs or values. For us, beliefs are guiding or organising principles for how we lead our lives. They act as filters for the information we receive from the world and thus help shape our perceptions. As such they act, as Anthony Robbins (1988) suggests, as 'models of possibility'.

In fact, the kind of things we believe at a given point have a direct impact on our actions, which in turn have a direct effect on our capacity to influence others.

Have you ever walked towards your classroom not looking forward to teaching your next lesson? How curious is this, as it hasn't actually happened yet? Are these thoughts in some way connected to your *belief* about what *might happen?* It's likely that the little voice in your head (you do talk to yourself, don't you? – we thought so!) has switched to a nagging and whiny tonality as you continue to process all the things that you *believe* will go wrong. When you arrive at the class and students are waiting for you, how easy is it to act according to what you know are agreed good practices? Do you, for example:

- Greet them with a smile and a 'good morning'?
- Congratulate the students who are lining up well?

Congruence

- Point out that you are pleased Maria is back from exclusion?
- Demonstrate enthusiasm for the lesson ahead?

Or possibly your responses lean towards the 'get your retaliation in first' approach?

At a pragmatic level, the huge advantage of considered and clearly defined beliefs is to provide us with built-in feedback within our own sensory system of how congruent or incongruent we are. For example, if we hold a genuine and embedded belief that people have a right to be treated with dignity and respect, then inevitably and valuably certain behaviours such as shouting, verbally intimidating students, sarcasm, to name but a few, are not only incompatible with this belief but will also *feel* uncomfortable. These uncomfortable feelings will lead us to withdraw from these behaviours when they occur. They will lead us to apologise or take other actions to minimise confrontation and rebuild and restore positive relationships. They will also provide the impetus to seek alternative strategies that not only promise the possibility of success but also generate actions that influence outcomes in the most positive, empowering and supportive way.

None of the above means that we become perfect human beings, remaining forever in emotional equilibrium and always highly upbeat and positive. We do not seek to deny the daily pressure we all face as teachers and the fallibility of being a human being. We will continue to make choices about our strategies for managing behaviour that on reflection we wish we hadn't made. The importance of strong beliefs is that it assists our ability to know the difference.

It is a simple truth that:

> *Everything we do and say will have an influence over the students in our classroom. We must therefore:*
> - *Ensure that our words and actions have a positive influence.*
> - *Take every opportunity to exert a positive influence.*
>
> Taken from *Strategies to Close the Learning Gap*
> (Hughes and Vass 2001)

We recommend that you take some time to reflect quietly on the things you believe about being a teacher and also the things you believe about being you at the times when you are at your best. To help you, we offer some beliefs that have guided and sustained us through our many years of teaching.

> *Never let the things that matter most be at the mercy of things that matter least.*
>
> Goethe

If what you are doing doesn't work – do something else

Apparently one of the clinical definitions of insanity is doing the same thing over and over again and expecting a different result each time. Our interpretation of this idea is simply that nothing works all the time with every student. There are no magic ideas, no panaceas or formulaic approaches to managing behaviour and creating positive relationships that will do the job for you. It makes sound sense that having more choice is considerably better than having less choice. In fact, generally speaking the person with the most options retains the most control over situations, especially if those options are used to move towards a win/win outcome.

The fact that you will use a simple direction and take-up time (see page 30) to bring Kyle back on task successfully but that five minutes later it doesn't have the same effect with Hayley isn't a reflection on the strategy. It simply means that other factors have kicked in. Some of these will be related to your choices – tone of voice, timing, etc. and some will have absolutely no connection to you – Hayley's been upset by another student or feels frustrated by the work and so on.

Having a plan B, C, D and sometimes Z makes it more likely you will call on an alternative strategy without being phased and use that strategy with calm assertion.

We have explained the rationale and offered an opportunity to clearly understand this point in Chapter 1. However, it is easier said than done. To increase your chances of making calmer and therefore more effective choices about your own behaviour, to be able to move smoothly round the secondary behaviours of sulking, sighing, 'it wasn't me!' type interactions, you also need some things to say and do that are well rehearsed, based on sound principles and have a strong probability of working. Within these chapters you will find many ideas to help you achieve this.

The only thing you can control in class is your own behaviour

This trips off the tongue quite easily and yet sometimes it is hard to achieve. It is undeniably true that when you talk to students about what makes an influential, well-respected teacher, the concept of respect shown to them is very high. Recent comments made to us by Year 11 students included:

Dignity and respect are fundamental rights

> *'She always seems to be pleasant and friendly.'*
> *'She talks to us like we're equal rather than some silly kid.'*
> *'Sometimes he gets wound up but he always says sorry.'*
> *'When they have a go at you it's for something you deserve but they don't bang on and on and they don't do it in front of your mates or make you feel small.'*

We feel that if you are genuinely congruent in this belief, you will model it far more than you don't. This also means that even at times of high challenge and stress such as exiting a student from class, it is important to stay as close as possible to this belief. There is a huge difference at emotional, intellectual, relational and physical levels between saying:

> *'OK Mike, you've chosen to be exited from the room. Take your work and go to Mrs Probin's class. You'll have a chance to explain when things are calmer. Go now, thanks'*

and saying:

> *'You just don't learn do you? I'm not prepared to waste time on you any more! Get out and go to Mrs Probin, maybe she can talk some sense into you.'*

What you say and how you say it creates an emotional response

This belief links closely with the previous one as you can see in the example above. Language, whether it is verbal or non-verbal, will *always* elicit a response at an emotional level. The important thing to remember therefore is that communication is never neutral and that people will place intent and motive on your words. A fuller explanation and practical approaches to choosing influential language patterns will be found in Chapter 3.

Teaching is about human transactions

Unfortunately, our experience tells us that the majority of training that teachers receive during ITT is focused on 'delivering' the curriculum. As consultants we are privileged enough to offer training to NQTs in many LEAs in the UK. When asked how much time was devoted directly to behaviour management training, the average answer is 1.5 hours. This sad statistic totally misses the point that 'delivery' is not what teachers do. Teachers teach! And teaching is about the micro-skill of human transaction. The significance of human transactions is best explained (if indeed explanation is necessary) by reference to the contrast between control and influence. You are aware from the beginning of this chapter that effective practitioners seek to establish and use their influence to create an appropriate learning climate. Now commit another statement to memory.

> **INFLUENCE IS ONLY POSSIBLE WHEN A CONNECTION EXISTS AT A HUMAN LEVEL**

Put simply, you cannot influence anybody from an emotional distance. You cannot influence someone by delivering a curriculum to them nor can you influence by inhibiting or placing barriers in the way of positive relationships. This is what we define as rapport. A useful vision of this rapport, which is so fundamental, comes from Anthony Robbins (1988) who defines it as,

> *'the ability to enter someone else's world . . . (so that we can) develop a relationship of responsiveness'.*

Effective teaching is skills-based

Effective teachers are those who have refined, tweaked and adjusted their skills over time to create habits and patterns of behaviour that engage and motivate *most* students *most* of the time. They have taken risks by stepping out of their particular comfort zones to try different ideas and strategies. They have reflected on their beliefs and they have absorbed the knowledge and information from the students they have taught to become even better. All of us as humans have mastered an enormous variety of highly complex skills to the point of unconscious competence – walking and talking are but two. Will you be the sort of teacher who has *x* years' experience or the sort that has one year's experience *x* times?

Without the relationship, skills are merely techniques and that is a very different state to be in. If you want a good illustration of the effective influence of techniques, think back to the phone call in a monotone voice that starts:

> *'Mr Vass? Good evening. This is purely a courtesy call. I'm not trying to sell you anything.'*

Could it be more obvious that the person on the phone is not only reading off a cue card but really does want to sell you something? In other words, they are employing techniques taught to them, but without the warmth of a relationship it just doesn't influence you to do anything other than switch off and hang up.

It is clearly desirable to manage student behaviour in class without damaging self-esteem – yours as well as theirs! A simple truth that we subscribe to is that the only way to nurture healthy self-esteem in children is to expose them to adults who have healthy self-esteem. It is accepted good practice that, when managing children's behaviours, whether we are acting in the role of teachers or parents, we should consider the impact of our actions on the self-esteem of the child. What is less commonly considered, and to our knowledge never taught in ITT and rarely in continuing professional development, is the maintenance of the adult's self-esteem. In *Creating Winning Classrooms* you will find a detailed perspective on the concepts and mechanics of self-esteem together with many practical strategies for use in class. However, Appendix A of this book approaches the issue of maintaining your own positive emotional states and offers a range of practical thoughts and ideas to support you in this.

Skills need to be developed within a relationship

Self-esteem is a primary goal

25

Questions for professional development

What do you feel about the topics covered in this chapter?

What are some of the implications of the topics within your classroom?

What do you think is the most important for you to remember from this chapter?

Chapter 3

The language of influence

Words call forth emotions and are universally the means by which we influence our fellow creatures.

Sigmund Freud

This chapter offers a wide range of opportunities to understand and develop your use of language to enhance your influence within your relationships with your students both in class and in following up on issues of concern. After explaining some fundamental ideas about the way in which language impacts on people, there is a collection of highly practical strategies and patterns for you to consider, rehearse and embed into your own work to enhance your influence in positive and beneficial ways.

Of all the strategies that you use to exert influence in developing a positive classroom climate characterised by healthy self-esteem and mutual respect, language provides the most potent of opportunities. In discussing language, we are clearly using the term to include non-verbal as well as verbal communication. However, it is important to recognise that language occurs privately inside our heads too in the form of internal dialogue or self-talk and in considering opportunities to influence we must include this form of language.

Before we explore the specific construction and use of influential language patterns, it is valuable to remind ourselves about some fundamental insights concerning language.

The impact of language

- Language of any sort is never neutral. Every piece of language you use will trigger an emotional response from those who hear it. As you have absolutely no choice in this happening, the question becomes therefore, is it your deliberate intent to generate a positive emotional response or a negative one? We would emphasise the notion of deliberate intent because we all have developed habits and patterns in our use of language, some of which are effective and some of which are not. Therefore, to elicit or influence a particular response from our students, it is necessary to be *consciously aware* (at least to start with) of what we are saying and how we are saying it. At a very simple level, contrast the possible responses that your students would have to these two sentences:

> *'We're having a test tomorrow.'*
> *'Tomorrow you will have an opportunity to show me what you understand about volcanoes.'*

- Recognise that you have the control and choice over how you use language and what language you use. Remember also that you should judge the impact and effectiveness of your communication by the *response* you get rather than what you *mean*. If, for example, we are attempting to calm a student down and it doesn't seem to be working, there is little point blaming the student. Rather, it is our responsibility to continue to alter how or what we are communicating in order to get closer to the desired outcome.
- Language does far more than communicate ideas and information – it actually shapes perceptions and beliefs. Our response to language is to use it to develop or reinforce an internal model of the world according to us! We tend to perceive and organise this model of the world by matching it to patterns that exist or for which we have accumulated enough evidence over time to make them true. Jack Canfield, one of the world's leading authors on the subject of self-esteem, says in his seminars:

> *'If one person calls you a horse, you will laugh and dismiss it. If ten people call you a horse you will consider a conspiracy. However, if a hundred people call you a horse, you will find yourself checking out the price of saddles!'*

On a more personal level, could it be true that you have been more sensitive or even 'prickly' to suggestions or advice offered when you have been feeling rather low or particularly tired? Have you looked for (and found) hidden criticism in well-meaning advice from someone you don't especially like or trust?

In other words, the language that we take in through our senses – hearing the actual words, interpreting the tonality and inflection and linking it to visual non-verbal cues such as posture etc. – is filtered and refined and matched to the thoughts, beliefs, values and a sense of self that we have. As you read further through this chapter, you will find practical examples of how language may deliberately be constructed to utilise this concept in order that your students feel empowered, confident and resilient rather than hurt, anxious and fragile in response to the way you communicate with them.

- Your choice of language to manage the classroom, particularly in response to inappropriate behaviour, can both reduce emotional arousal and be calming and defusing or it can have an incendiary effect like throwing petrol on a bonfire. A key question therefore becomes, 'How do you make those choices?' Remember E + R = O from Chapter 1? What has to happen to increase ('tweak') your ability to choose the calming and defusing option *even more* than you do already?

We refer to these as 'core' skills not because they are any more important than any of the others but because they tend to be features of other ways of using language in the sense that they underpin or add value to the things you say in class. These are common threads, which all successful discipline transactions with pupils contain.

Whatever the specific language strategy you use, work to build these skills into it until you become unconsciously skilled at them.

The pause

It takes time to stop doing something and think about, understand and then do something else. You are more likely to achieve compliance if you deliberately allow time for this process. Putting a pause after you call the pupil's name and before you give the direction helps to gain and then sustain the attention. It's also OK to have to repeat a pupil's name a couple of times.

The vast majority of pupils respond to their name by giving you eye contact, which allows you to add assertive eye contact and refocusing gestures to the directions.

On those rare occasions when pupils don't look up (and you know they understand the language), speak to the ears. Getting involved in power struggles that involve the, *'look at me when I'm talking to you!'* are doomed from the outset.

It's worth remembering that the style, inflection and tonality you use to call someone's name will have a direct bearing on their mood when they give you eye contact.

Give positive directions

Most people are aware of the concept that positive language is more effective than negative language. So how come significant numbers of directions to students that we witness being given to students are negative? By negative, we mean directions, which revolve around 'don't'.

'Don't call out, please'; 'Don't push. You'll all get a go.'

This particular language pattern is a good example of why consciously *understanding* why something is effective supports our development of the strategy.

'Don't think of something blue NOW.'

The reason why following this instruction is nearly impossible is that the word 'don't' doesn't exist except as a sound or a squiggle on a page. It has no sensory experience in that you can't touch, taste, feel or see a 'don't'. Your brain goes to the only thing that it hears that it can pattern match to – something blue. Once you have done that, it becomes difficult not to think about it.

Reframing your language to use more 'do' directions has the advantage of:

- Focusing on a successful alternative rather than a mistake
- Giving people a strategy for being successful
- Offering a clarity of purpose
- Working with how the brain processes language.

Does this mean that you will never say 'don't' again? We don't think so! Simply consider deliberate ways in which your language can become positive.

'*Don't run*' becomes '*Walking, please.*'

'*Don't call out*' becomes '*Hands up*' or '*One at a time.*'

Use 'take-up time'

Imagine asking a pupil to '*Face this way with your bag on the floor, thanks*' and then continuing to stare at them until they had completed the direction in every detail. Or maybe you've been asked a question at a staff meeting and been aware of everybody looking at you. Comfortable?

The image we use is of a spotlight lighting up a pupil each time you call their name and speak to them. If we are refocusing a pupil's behaviour, the longer the spotlight stays on, the greater the potential for feeling discomfort. Further or extended eye contact can also be construed as a challenge.

Turning away and breaking eye contact when you are up front in class or moving away as you are working the room is a subtle yet very powerful way of conveying:

1. The transaction is over and there's no more to be said.
2. You are confident that the pupil will follow the direction.
3. You expect them to comply.
4. You care about their self-esteem and will turn the spotlight off quickly.
5. You do not dwell or add emotional 'heat' to your directions.

Take-up time also fulfils two other crucial purposes:

1. It gives time and space for pupils to do what they need within the 4Rs framework (see Chapter 4) to sort out their emotional baggage. Some pupils will just do it but some will sigh exaggeratedly, walk as slowly as they can back to their seat, or look around at their friends and shrug or raise their eyes to the ceiling as if to say, '*What's her problem? I wasn't doing anything.*' To a confident and influential classroom leader this is not a direct challenge, just an example of secondary behaviours and dealt with best by ignoring it.
2. By moving into and out of a discipline transaction as quickly as possible and then making a point of speaking or going to a pupil who is on task, or reclaiming the lesson if you are up front, you are giving a powerful message that gains additional power every time you do it. The message is that greater attention will be devoted to pupils who work within the accepted framework.

The language of choice

The notion of choice is a fundamental component of influence as we have explored more fully in both *Confident Classroom Leadership* and *Creating Winning Classrooms*. We revisit the concept in Chapter 4 in addressing how the nine core principles extend and enhance your ability to positively influence.

However, as a language pattern in its own right, the language of choice is crucial. At the heart of its impact is the message we gave in Chapter 1 – you can't *make* students do things. Therefore, making clear and explicit in your directions to them that they are responsible and accountable for the behaviours they choose offers a fundamental level of influence. Namely, that you not only recognise the ineffectiveness of, but also will actively avoid, the confrontational language driven by the *'I must win'*, *'I can't let them get away with that'* mindset.

It may seem unduly simplistic to suggest that when faced with inappropriate behaviour, using patterns such as:

> *'Jack (pause), if you choose to continue talking then you will be choosing a warning'*

will be effective. However, our experience and the overwhelming feedback from teachers in all phases that we have trained indicate that indeed it is hugely influential. It is, of course, entirely in keeping with the ideas explained in Chapter 1 since it seeks to influence directly the consequences part of the ABC model. In other words, the student will make a choice and you will *manage* the consequences of that choice rather than fruitlessly try to *control* the behaviour itself.

Non-verbal congruence

It may seem an obvious statement but in the event of any mismatch between your verbal and non-verbal repertoire, students will pick up first on the non-verbal component. A core skill is therefore to ensure that whatever influential language pattern you use is matched by calm, non-hostile posture and that tonality is suitably assertive where necessary without being aggressive.

Here are three key reasons to avoid confrontational behaviour management.

- It doesn't work.
- If we use it, it not only models it but legitimises our pupils using it.
- It damages self-esteem and many of your pupils will be vulnerable already in this area. This directly impacts on how comfortably students can trust you and trust is an essential component of influence.

If what we do makes pupils feel threatened or they perceive that this is happening, they will react within their more primitive, reptilian brain – the fight or flight response and the influence we are effecting will be towards feelings of hostility, defiance and self-preservation at all costs.

None of these outcomes is compatible with positive and empowering classrooms. In many cases the flight will be internalised and although the pupils will not physically flee (although some do), they will feel powerless, hurt and disabled by the stress this brings.

The fight is clearly undesirable but is a natural response to the perception of threat. By actually doing something like answering back, arguing and other verbal challenges pupils are actually reducing their own levels of stress.

Confrontation can be perceived from many angles:

- Tone of voice
- Leaning over a seated pupil
- Standing too close (like boxers before a contest)
- Moving quickly towards a pupil
- Finger wagging and in some cases prodding
- Banging desks
- Hands on hips and leaning forward.

It makes sense to develop ways of acting, believing and thinking that support behaviours in you that are more helpful and positively influential.

Thank you

We have found it is easier to implement the ideas above by using the simple skill of saying 'thank you' after giving a direction and before using take-up time. When you read formal letters requesting you to do things they often finish by saying:

'Thank you in anticipation of your cooperation.'

This is the verbal equivalent and strongly reinforces the idea below.

Act 'as if'

The expectation of compliance is vital to classroom management. Effective teachers work very hard to behave in a way that gives a congruent message that they are confident the pupil will see the reasonable nature of their request without feeling attacked personally and will cooperate with them.

At its simplest this means that all your behaviour management strategies will be far more influential if you *expect* them to work.

Agreement frames

One of the most rapid and effective ways of exerting influence in a beneficial way is to elicit a state of agreement from another person.

Agreement in this case is represented by a sense of being connected or understood by another person rather than necessarily believing exactly the same things. How is this sense of connection or empathy achieved? If you refer to things that people:

- know to be true
- would like to be true
- can verify through their senses as true

you will generate that sense of agreement.

Well-trained salespersons use something called a 'yes set'. They begin to connect and establish rapport with a potential customer by asking questions or making statements that the person can agree to.

'Are you happy just looking around for now?'
'At least you've got out of the rain for a while.'
'You'll let me know when you need some help?'

This is not only relaxing (because agreement means no conflict) but it also begins to establish a pattern of trust and agreement.

Maybe . . . and . . .

Probably our favourite agreement frame is the *'maybe . . . and . . .'* pattern. 'Maybe . . . and . . .' is a hugely effective response to secondary behaviours and has the effect of not only reducing emotional arousal but also refocusing the agenda back to work. Secondary behaviours, as a quick reminder of something we first mentioned in *Confident Classroom Leadership*, are those things people do to deflect or avoid the *'heat'* of getting caught out doing something wrong. The 'secondary' part indicates the sequence of behaviours. Primary behaviours are the things you will correct and often the student's response will be to deflect the issue by introducing something unrelated. Here's an example.

> Teacher: *'Kyle* (pause), *and Damien* (pause) *. . . pens down and facing this way, thanks.'*
> Damien: (exasperated tonality) *'I was only asking him what page we were on* (sigh).'
> Teacher: *'Maybe you were, Damien, and I need you to face this way. This information will help you. Thanks.'*

Obviously the teacher will choose to ignore the fact that she knows Damien was doing nothing of the sort. She also chooses to ignore the provocative tonality and sighing. She recognises that any attention given to these issues will concede the agenda (and therefore the influence) to Damien.

How does it work? The word 'maybe' is an agreement. It makes Damien correct in his belief *and* it doesn't make the teacher incorrect. In the reality of the situation, it doesn't really matter what Damien was or wasn't talking about. It doesn't matter whether he believes he was doing the right thing or not. What matters is getting his attention so that the 'flow' of the lesson is not interrupted. When Damien hears the word 'maybe', he is subconsciously thinking and justifying his comments with *internal* dialogue that runs something like this:

> *'Yeah, well, I <u>was</u> asking about the page. Just as long as you understand that, it's OK.'*

In other words, he and the teacher agree. If they agree then no conflict exists, no further defensive postures are required and it becomes easier to follow the next instruction, i.e. respond to the primary behaviour and pay attention (after all, it's no big deal really).

Contrast the above with the following:

> *'That's not true, Damien, because you were talking about the match last night. Why lie? Now face this way and LISTEN!'*

If you were Damien, it is unlikely you would be saying to yourself,

> *'OK. Fair enough. I was lying. I'd better make a good choice and listen to my teacher now so I can learn lots.'*

Please recognise the significance of the word 'and' in this transaction. Some people have suggested the word 'but' is equally effective. This is not true.

> *'I agree with everything you have said so far BUT . . .'*

It doesn't take psychic powers to recognise that disagreement, criticism or discord is about to happen. In other words, no agreement actually exists at all.

When students feel validated in their perspective, the emotional arousal caused by the need to defend your point of view is removed. Low emotional arousal allows rational responses and increases the possibility of instructions being followed.

Mind reading

In developing your ability to empathise with students' feelings you can make some accurate assumptions about the emotions they *might* be experiencing. You can use this information to construct an agreement frame.

Imagine you keep a student back at the end of the lesson to talk about some behaviour that was inappropriate. Are they looking forward to it? Will they be expecting an empowering and pleasant experience? Or might they be marginally aggrieved? Mind reading allows us to use this information to generate positive influence on the emotional state of the student before we address the issue of behaviour.

> Teacher: *'Thanks for staying back. I imagine you're a bit annoyed at missing part of break and it's important that you have a chance to explain to me what went on.'*

The student's response will be similar to the 'maybe', i.e. they will begin to agree – internally only – that this is indeed how they are feeling. Because this is correct, there is every possibility that the next part can also be true for them. Hence we have the potential for resolution rather than conflict simply by the influence of our choice of language.

Motivational feedback

Sometimes the use of praise doesn't seem to impact as powerfully as we would hope it to. On occasions it may seem patronising to students and in reality there are only so many ways of saying 'well done' with sincerity. Agreement frames can give us the edge because they offer powerful ways to trigger internal or intrinsic motivation in others by the language patterns we use.

As a general rule, when you give feedback to students about their work, start by describing in a non-judgemental way the parts that are competent.

> *'Let's see Jenny. You've organised your ideas into paragraphs, some spellings have been corrected and I can see you've used several quotes.'*

While you are making these observations the student is able to nod along with you either internally or externally (it helps to actually point at them). From this position of agreement, you are now able to add ideas or suggestions that would boost self-esteem and the student's own beliefs about her capability.

> *'You've kept a positive attitude going on this, I bet. I imagine you're pleased with this, eh Jenny? Give it a final proofread and I'll look forward to seeing the final copy.'*

The student will easily and comfortably accept this second part of the teacher's conversation because it has flowed naturally and seamlessly from information that was demonstrably true. Notice that the teacher's comments are speculative rather than definitive. Keeping a curious tone in the voice, using *'I bet'* and turning the comment about being pleased into a question encourage the student to accept them as true. In this way, the teacher has allowed the student to make judgements about herself that add to her sense of worth and competence as a learner. She has accepted evidence of competence and capability as a learner. This way is infinitely more potent than:

> *'Excellent! You've done a good job on this. I'm pleased with you.'*

There is absolutely nothing wrong with this type of feedback. It is simple to give and in the vast majority of cases will trigger a sense of well-being.

All we are suggesting is that offering motivational feedback through agreement frames helps to build and sustain powerful belief systems within students regarding their capability. As such, it adds choice and therefore extends our ability to usefully influence the emotional state of students in our classes.

Presuppositions

A language presupposition is a statement that contains assumptions, which must be accepted as true in order for the statement to make sense. For example:

'Are you still doing your best to positively influence children's lives?'

contains the assumption that up until now that's exactly what you have been doing. If you respond to the question, you accept the presupposition.

Influential communication utilises presuppositions in many ways. A useful idea is to presuppose the things you would like to happen.

'How pleased are you with this work?'

presupposes that you will be pleased to some degree. Even the response *'Not very pleased'* indicates *some* satisfaction.

Here are some other examples:

'What do you need to remember about diagrams/using scissors safely/tidying up, etc.?'

This presupposes that the student knows the answer and will be able to make a more successful choice. It has a significantly more empowering influence than:

'What have you forgotten about . . . ?'

Work out the presuppositions contained in these statements. When you have done this successfully, consider where you will use them most effectively.

How easy has it been to . . .? (it's been easy)
I wonder who will ask the first question? (there will be questions)
When will you feel that you have understood this topic? (you will understand)
How quickly will we get organised into our groups?
Do you want to do the assignment before the practical or after?
Next time you try this, it will be easier.
Which bit of the example is bothering you at the moment?
When you've calmed down, I can listen to your side of the story.
Can you tell me how soon you'll finish this?
How confident are you about the coursework?
As you read this book you realise you have more skills than ever before. These ideas will help you to become even better.

Now, how many examples can you think of? For now, limit yourself to four or five.

Of course, not all presuppositions empower or positively enhance relationships. Because we generally accept the presupposition contained in statements without conscious challenge, some of the comments we direct to students, although without any harmful intent, can provide evidence that further damages often vulnerable self-esteem.

Statement	Presupposition
What have you done this time?	It's always you!
I want the truth now.	LIAR!
How many times do you need telling?	THICKO!
You again!	It's only what I expect of you.
See you can behave when you try.	You're not as disturbed as I thought.
I'm just wasting my breath.	I give up on you.
You haven't stuck to your plan today.	You're a failure.
This morning was OK but . . .	That doesn't count because you screwed up this afternoon.
Believe it or not I'm one of the few people who are on your side.	The others hate you!
What else could you add to the picture?	It isn't good enough.
No, that's not it (in response to student answering your question).	Don't be silly. THINK!

Figure 3.1 Presuppositions that may wound self-esteem

Escalator language

We first came across the term and the concept of 'escalator language' through exploring the work of an amazing therapist and author called Bill O'Hanlon. We liked the image of the escalator as representing forward and upward movement as a normal and automatic process. Bill works with clients in ways that create possibilities for a future they would prefer. In doing so he uses language in ways that suggest that goals will be achieved or things will become easier.

They imply that any difficulty encountered is merely a phase or stage to be negotiated and in that way dilute or remove the idea of being 'stuck' or 'locked into a particular outcome'. It occurred to us that this principle is enormously valid in building confidence, boosting motivation and enhancing self-esteem with all the students in our classrooms, not just those who are experiencing the most difficulty.

In offering the possibility of progress or improvement to students, these patterns of language are often characterised by the use of temporal expressions such as:

yet, so far, up to this point, until now, recently, sometimes, from time to time, occasionally or by expressions that minimise the scale of the difficulty:

bit, just, only, quite, most, little

By implication, the student has achieved something already and is connected to the possibility of being even more successful.

Consider the impact on your students when you use comments like the ones below. You can think, can you not, of specific children who would 'grow' as a result of receiving feedback in these ways?

> *'OK, Jake, which bit isn't quite clear for you yet?'*
> *'Up until now this topic has been a challenge.'*
> *'Just finish the diagram and then we'll change the activity.'*
> *'It's true that some parts of the lesson haven't gone as well as others.'*
> *'It's only the graph that's a bit tricky.'*
> *'Kyle, I notice you haven't opened your book yet.'*
> *'You've met most of your targets completely.'*
> *'Up to this point you've felt just a little frustrated by this topic.'*

Connecting language to learning

Most teachers are aware now of the differences in learning styles that exist. There is a wealth of books available that detail how VAK (visual, auditory and kinaesthetic) learning preferences can be supported and encouraged so that students can learn in the ways that suit them best. For a highly pragmatic approach to these ideas and a range of actual strategies, we would recommend *Strategies to Close the Learning Gap* (Hughes and Vass 2001).

Presenting as many opportunities as possible for students to process information in ways that they feel most comfortable with is an essential component of curriculum and lesson planning as it will influence the success students experience. A further source of influence is available in the way you can structure language to engage and connect with these styles of information processing.

When we talk about our experiences, we use many phrases that are certainly not random but instead relate to particular senses or ways of thinking and processing that we are experiencing at the time. In other words the phrases connect with and represent visual, auditory and kinaesthetic processing.

These are just a few examples of common phrases:

Visual	Auditory	Kinaesthetic
I see what you mean	It sounds dodgy to me	This feels tough
It's not clear	That rings a bell	Hold on a minute
I'm in the dark over this	It's unheard of	Can you handle this?
This is dull	Tell me what to do	I don't follow
It's just dawned on me	You're on the right wavelength	Can't put my finger on it

Figure 3.2 Examples of sensory-based language

How does this help? Well, as part of the big picture the ideas described in detail above may well help you to press home any positive influence you have. Alternatively, you may feel it's too much hassle or the ideas are a bit heavy going for you. In which case you may well be thinking that it's all mumbo jumbo and that it doesn't offer a glimmer of light at the end of the tunnel.

See what we mean yet?

Students in your class will make sense of whatever is going on through the VAK senses. If you are using a range of predicates to complement their own thinking, you will connect more fully and communicate with them more effectively, which just happen to be the two main criteria for influence.

'But I still can't grasp the relevance. It doesn't sound the sort of stuff I could use in MY class!'

See if this example helps to clarify things. Let's eavesdrop on a conversation in class and hope it touches a nerve.

Student: *'Mr Vass, I don't get it. Can you show me again?'*
Teacher: *'I have actually told you twice before. Please listen carefully this time'* (note the presupposition).
Student: *'I did listen! I just don't see what you're on about!'*
Teacher: *'OK, pay attention. I want you to give me an account of how the poet has used these verses to describe being different from others.'*

The student clearly needs some visual response to the request *'Can you show me again?'* By tuning in to this, the teacher could respond with matching language such as:

'We'll look at these stanzas. Then within these stanzas, I'd like you to imagine these words highlighted in some way, almost as if they flash or glow. The poet is using these words to paint a picture of how he feels being an immigrant in this country. I'd like to see written down, your thoughts on how he feels. You might like to imagine him being ignored and insulted and visualise his face at the time. That may give you a clue to start you off.'

Questions for professional development

What do you feel about the topics covered in this chapter?

What are some of the implications of the topics within your classroom?

What do you think is the most important for you to remember from this chapter?

Chapter 4

Nine core principles

Centering [sic] on principles provides . . . power to communicate and
cooperate even under conditions of stress and fatigue.'
                    Dr Stephen Covey, *Principle Centred Leadership*

As you consider the quote above, it may become clear that it is no coin-
cidence that the conditions of 'stress and fatigue' referred to are invari-
ably the times that our decisions about our use of strategies are likely
to become less effective with the inevitable result that our interactions
with students can tend to be more irritable or even confrontational. In
what ways, then, do principles help us to stay true to our ideals and
allow us to remain connected intellectually and emotionally to our
understanding and experiences of good practice? This chapter seeks
to provide some answers to this question as well as offering nine principles that we believe to be at the heart of effective classroom management.

The work of Stephen Covey (see References) has had a significant
influence not just on our practice but crucially also on our understanding of what helps teachers to become effective and to sustain that
effectiveness. In this chapter we attempt to interpret some of our
understandings within an educational context and show how this
leads us to develop the nine core principles that form the basis of this
chapter.

In September 2000, we were involved as consultants in a national
project developing training materials on behaviour management on
behalf of the Department for Education and Employment (as they
were then known). The materials were published and distributed to
every LEA in England. At the heart of the materials were the nine core
principles given below.

A consistent element of the feedback to the materials was the value of
articulating key principles that all teachers could relate to not only on
a pragmatic level but also in a more fundamental way in the sense of
providing organising beliefs to engage with that practice.

*Nine core
principles*

- Plan for good behaviour
- Work within the 4Rs framework
- Separate the (inappropriate) behaviour from the child
- Use the language of choice
- Keep the focus on primary behaviours
- Actively build trust and rapport
- Model the behaviour you wish to see
- Always follow up on issues that count
- Work to repair and restore relationships.

The understanding and adoption of guiding principles in your work with young people will provide you, we believe, with a foundation that sustains the choices you make about relationships, behaviours and beliefs that result in positive and emotionally empowering classrooms built on respect and trust.

In all our workshops, we are at pains to emphasise that there are no 'quick fix' answers to managing student behaviours positively. Nor are there instant actions that somehow magically create empowering classroom climates. That is not to say that there are no additional strategies and skills that all of us, whatever our experience, can learn, rehearse and embed into our practice that will support us in our goal of effective classroom management. However, what is important is that the development of skill needs to be balanced or grounded within the sincerity of principle.

Covey describes principles as 'natural laws' in the sense that they are at work and have influence on us whether or not we are aware of them. He cites basic principles such as fairness, honesty, trust and justice, integrity and equity as being highly influential in a positive interpersonal way when present and equally influential, but in a destructive or disconnected way when absent from human transactions.

Working from the perspective of well-defined, personally understood and meaningful principles forms the basis of modelling what it is you wish to receive back in terms of relationships and responses from your students. Principles provide the security that allows you to be at your best more often, since your security is not derived from the reactions to you or others' beliefs about you.

In essence, therefore, principles supply the rationale or 'why' behind the interpersonal transactions with our students, which even as the nature and context of these transactions changes, will remain constant. In this way the variety of skills and strategies we call upon to manage our classrooms become the actions or 'what' of the transactions. As no single strategy is successful in every context, there is an inherent need to extend and develop the choices of strategy open to us – to increase the tools in the bag, as it were, in order to be more responsive and flexible. The likelihood of developing and refining strategies for ourselves that have the possibility of being effective is significantly increased when they emerge from the constant of our principles.

We genuinely believe that these nine principles encompass those 'natural laws' to which Covey refers. As you read our thinking about them together with the practical applications of them, we invite you to make connections with the contexts of your own experience and just see how they will be useful to you in your work.

In an environment that may have 30 or more slightly differing agendas, good behaviour does not occur accidentally. Nor is it the outcome of wishing and hoping. Socially appropriate, mutually respectful behaviours occur within established boundaries, which in turn emanate from a deliberate and conscious planning.

Plan for good behaviour

Entering a classroom with little or no idea of what you intend to teach, how you intend to teach, what resources you have available and how best to utilise them is not a model for comfort. This is why teachers are usually meticulous in their curriculum component of lesson planning. However, every teacher also knows with reasonable certainty that behaviour that does nothing to enhance learning *will occur.* Whether this is on the lower end of the continuum such as arriving late and not having equipment or at the top end with significant verbal and even physical abuse occurring (or indeed anywhere in between), it makes little sense to enter a classroom without adequate preparation and planning. Planning for good behaviour should be as considered and rigorous as planning for the curriculum.

Think of the last time you were in class and a student behaved in a way that didn't fit in with your lesson plan. Was your response or redirection calm and considered? Did you reclaim the agenda and refocus on the flow of the lesson with minimum fuss? Well, you probably did because that's what happens a lot of the time. However, there are also times for all of us when reclaiming the agenda occurs after what Daniel Goleman (1996) refers to as *'emotional hijacking'* (see Chapter 6). In other words, we respond from a more adversarial or aggressive perspective as a result of rational thinking (i.e. our knowledge of what constitutes good practice) being overtaken by the more basic survival thinking of 'fight or flight'.

These instances of behaviour management occur when the high level of emotional arousal seems to connect directly to our mouths as we interact with the student(s) in what Bill Rogers (1994) describes so aptly as the *'guts to gob'* style of behaviour management.

Our experience of having worked with many hundreds of schools around the UK suggests to us that this reactive style of behaviour management is not in the least bit uncommon. However, in our calmer, more rational moments the majority of teachers would accept that the *'guts to gob'* approach not only doesn't work, it almost always escalates the situation and makes it far worse! A fuller explanation of why this is so can be found in both Chapters 5 and 6 although for now, the simple truth is that the worst possible time to construct a suitable response is actually while the emotional arousal is high, i.e. at the time of the verbal exchange.

For this reason alone, our goal in planning for good behaviour should be to be highly proactive in those parts of the classroom dynamic over

43

which we have elements of control – the antecedents – mentioned in Chapter 1. This means that a significant focus of our planning for good behaviour should be on preventative strategies. Put simply:

'What is it you <u>deliberately</u> do that is designed to minimise the likelihood of poor behaviour occurring?'

---

1. Make a list of as many things that you already do, have heard of or know about as fit into the category of preventative practice. Be aware that these will impact at least at these different levels:
   - Organisationally – seating plans etc.
   - Intellectually – differentiating work, learning styles, etc.
   - Emotionally – meeting and greeting students.
2. When you have temporarily exhausted your list, get colleagues from your department or key stage to add to your list.
3. Ask as many colleagues in school, including non-teaching staff, to contribute.
4. Place a copy of the list as it stands so far in your planner or other accessible place.
5. Refer to it frequently to:
   a) affirm your existing good practice and
   b) try something else if required.
6. Add to it each time you connect with a new idea.

In summary then, the principle of planning for good behaviour allows you to create opportunities for your students to succeed with their relationships with each other and with you. It reduces the opportunities for or indeed likelihood of conflict and supports a climate of emotional stability. If you are maximising the opportunities for others to feel calm and successful, you will in turn feel more satisfied, less stressed and derive increased satisfaction and feelings of competence from your work. Planning helps you to retain perspective on events, develop purpose and prioritise.

Of course, because you are working with people, no matter how proactive you are in prevention, you cannot legislate for every eventuality or range of emotions students bring with them to class and the unexpected will happen. The important question at this point is:

'How do I respond to these events so that their impact is minimised rather than escalated?'

In other words, how do you avoid getting to the 'guts to gob' reaction that inevitably makes things worse? In *Creating Winning Classrooms*, we discussed the concept of proactivity and how valuable it is in creating more of what you want from experience. In simple terms then, to avoid 'guts to gob', you have to make a decision to actually *do something* that takes you in a different direction completely whether that direction is a physical, emotional or intellectual one. It is the next principle that comes into its own to support your choices of direction in these circumstances.

We have discussed and explained the idea of the 4Rs in other books, each time from a slightly different perspective. We make no apology for a brief revisit here simply because the application and use of the 4Rs goes way beyond an idea or a concept. It is actually a way of guiding your thinking and behaviours in class and as such it not only fits entirely with the 'natural law' idea of a principle but also gives you things to believe, say and do that move you comfortably away from 'guts to gob'.

Work within the 4Rs framework

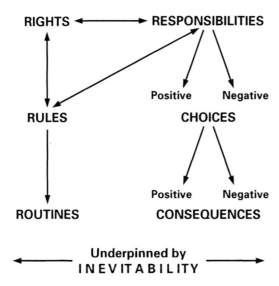

Figure 4.1 The 4Rs

Join us in a conceptual and insightful 'walk' around the 4Rs.

Rights

The concept of rights is incredibly powerful and we believe it is at the heart of how teachers respond to students. In our view, there is a direct correlation between the degree to which certain rights are infringed and the degree to which we respond as teachers. It seems a rational way of explaining how you can walk past a group of students in the corridor and feel comfortable interpreting the low level of jostling or banter as 'harmless fun' but further along some sense leads you to intervene with another situation.

Having discussed these ideas with teachers around the UK, there seems to be universal acknowledgement within the profession that there are (at least) four basic rights that pertain.

- Your right to teach
- Your students' right to learn
  (Naturally, these are interchangeable between teachers and students.)
- Everybody's right to safety (physical and psychological)
- Everybody's right to be treated with dignity and respect.

It may come as no surprise that when we have asked students of different ages around the country questions about what they *should* be allowed to do or have protected in school, they come up with the same list as teachers.

The significance of this is that despite tensions that do exist between adults and students in schools, there is also some valuable common ground. This vital area of shared goals as to how we would all like to be treated is a constructive and important platform for building relationships since working in this way inherently offers the notion of win/win.

Responsibilities

However, rights that are not coupled to responsibilities have considerably less impact and strength. As teachers, it is vital that we keep rights and responsibilities connected. This means being absolutely overt and explicit in sustaining the bottom line message of:

You don't enjoy your rights at the expense of other people's rights.

If you have a right to be treated with respect then your responsibility is to treat others the same way. It is crucial to emphasise the mutuality of these rights.

Choices

The challenge we face, especially working with adolescents, is how to generate the concept of taking responsibility for one's actions. The key to this process is the notion of choice. People *choose* their behaviours. One of the features of being a human being is the fact that between stimulus and response we have a choice. Remember $E + R = O$?

Consider the last time in your life when you felt or said to yourself that you had 'no choice'. As you remember that occasion, can you recall being overwhelmed by a sense of hope, joy and boundless optimism for the future? No? We suggest, then, that there was a strong chance that you were struck by a sense of irritation, frustration and feeling powerless. That is the emotional impact of choice or the lack of it. Anyone who is a parent will be aware of the challenge of giving children choices because it is inevitable they will make choices that you don't want them to or which are inappropriate.

Consequences

Fortunately, every time we make a choice, there is a consequence. Even choosing to do nothing brings the consequence that things remain the same. In life, many resultant consequences are natural events. Eat too much and you put on weight and so on. Within school, however, the consequences are largely constructed and therefore artificial. Even so, we must do our best to keep them as close to the features of natural consequences as possible. As you construct and use consequences, consider these questions:

- Are they fair?
- Are they reasonable, i.e. matched to the event?
- Are they in the person's best interests in terms of helping them make more useful choices?
- Are they related as far as possible to the event so the connection is obvious?
- Are they largely known or predictable so people can make informed choices?

The relationship between choices and consequences needs to be one of inevitability rather than severity. In this way, consequences have impact and are highly influential. There is a common misconception that positive consequences (rewards) are the opposites of negative consequences (sanctions). This view is completely false. Rewards and sanctions are actually the same thing. They are both consequences that *result directly from the student's choice.*

Our very firm belief is that unless as teachers we approach things from this perspective, we are not holding students accountable for their actions. We are allowing them to opt out of responsibility and disconnect themselves from this important relationship. This is not simply the case of inappropriate behaviour we are talking about here. It is vital too that when students make good choices we help them to consciously recognise the fact that they have made a choice. Encouraging students to recognise their good choices is an extremely effective way of creating empowerment and makes a significant contribution to positive self-esteem.

Rewards and sanctions

The relationship is therefore this. When students make good choices, we offer them rewards – most usually in the form of low-level social approval such as smiles, nods, thumbs up, verbal praise, etc. – that in themselves will significantly contribute towards the students' sense of belonging. Of course, the rewards continuum extends through a wide range of other reinforcing practices such as written comments, notes home, displaying work and other more formal celebrations of certificates and so on.

When, however, they make poor choices in the sense of being outside the 4Rs framework, it is also crucial that some form of sanction follows with inevitability. Again, this doesn't have to be more than social disapproval in the first instance such as frowning, shakes of the head, verbal redirections, but will also include elements from your formal hierarchy of sanctions such as warnings and moving seat through to loss of privilege and time including detentions.

Here comes the whole crux of the dynamic, which gives both credibility and impact to the use of rewards and sanctions. Again, we ask you to commit something to memory:

SANCTIONS <u>LIMIT</u> BEHAVIOUR
REWARDS <u>CHANGE</u> BEHAVIOUR

Sanctions serve as a limit to behaviour. They are the metaphorical brick walls into which students run and halt. It is only when we acknowledge or recognise the effort they put in on the way to picking themselves up and having another go at getting it right that behaviour begins to change.

> *Having given Clint a choice about settling down to work or choosing to sit at a table on his own, Mrs Hook moves away giving 'take-up time' and leaving Clint to make his choice. She also begins to give attention to Kyle who is having a go at the work. Clint continues to talk loudly to the student next to him thus indicating his choice. Mrs Hook responds to the choice Clint makes:*
>
> *'I see you've chosen to sit here on your own, Clint. Choose to bring your work and sit here now. Thanks.'*
>
> *Clint huffs, mutters under his breath and eventually with much bluster and bravado sits in the seat indicated. He is no longer talking loudly but is sulking. He is also not yet on task.*
>
> *Mrs Hook recognises that this is a key time. She could ignore him because he isn't doing <u>exactly</u> what he should be doing. However, this just emphasises and extends the sanction. Instead, Mrs Hook walks over to Clint, engages him with a smile and says:*
>
> *'Thanks for choosing to settle down. Can I help you get started?'*
>
> *In this simple and highly effective exchange she is unambiguously letting Clint know that no grudges are held by this teacher and that although she will correct his behaviour and follow through with his choice she will also notice the efforts he makes, however small, to make amends. In Mrs Hook's class there is always a way back to being successful.*

One of the questions that sometimes arises in our workshops when we discuss the notion of inevitability with rewards and sanctions is:

> *What about the students who just do most of the things they are expected to? Should you reward and recognise them <u>just</u> for doing what's expected of them?*

The answer to this is very simple: YES!

Those small signs of social recognition – smiles, nods, etc. will not only deepen these students' sense of belonging, they will reinforce to the rest of the class the behaviours that lead to success in your classroom.

If no one acknowledged or even commented on the things that you do that are expected of you, would you mind? Would there be a possibility that you would feel ignored or taken for granted? This is largely a rhetorical question of course but it is worth remembering that children feel the same way.

Rules

In our view, it is only when the concepts outlined above are clearly articulated and firmly embedded, that the concept of rules makes logical sense. We have explained this idea in more detail in *Confident Classroom Leadership* but we believe that rules are easier to endorse and accept when they relate directly to the rights mentioned. In other words the message we give to students is that the rules exist to protect the things that they would like to have. It is important therefore to create that link in the formulation of rules or codes of conduct. Ideally, a linguistic connection should be present. For example, variations on the rule, *'To protect all our safety, there is no swearing, name-calling or put-downs in our class'*, exist in most classes. However, by including a right within the rule you are making that clear connection.

Routines

Routines can be viewed as the regular practices that we should proactively teach students (rather than tell then assume they know) to help make events run smoothly. This will take the form of entry and exit from classrooms to accessing resources, going to assembly and many, many more.

So there you have a brief reprise of the 4Rs framework. At this point you may be experiencing some mild confusion because earlier on we said that the 4Rs as a principle was a highly powerful set of ideas, which actually offered pragmatic support in taking you away from the emotional hijacking of the 'guts to gob' phenomenon to a state where rational thought and calmly delivered good practice was the order of the day. Alright, you've understood the 4Rs but cannot see how it is so practically helpful yet.

The key to unlocking the influence of the 4Rs lies with language. As we have pointed out, language does far more than communicate information. It actually conveys concepts, triggers an emotional response and is fundamental in shaping our beliefs and perceptions. In taking and using the *language* of the 4Rs framework you actually have things to say and ways of saying them that:

- are based on sound principles
- are grounded in fairness
- actively reduce emotional arousal because they act as rehearsed 'scripts'.

Here are a few of the language patterns associated with the 4Rs.

4Rs language	Common language
How does that fit with my right to be treated with respect?	*Don't be rude. How dare you speak to me that way?*
If you choose to keep talking then you'll be choosing to sit on your own.	*I've told you before – stop talking or I'll move you over there.*
What's our rule for asking questions? (Pleasant voice) That's right – hands up. Use it next time, thanks.	*Don't call out. How many more times?*
I can see you need to make your point. When I've finished this then I'll listen. The consequence of choosing to argue now will be I'll ask you to wait outside.	*I'm not arguing with you. If you don't stop you'll be outside the room.*

Figure 4.2 Some 4Rs language examples

The best way of seeing how effective this way of talking is would be to say each conversation out loud and notice the difference in feeling you associate with each one. Pay attention also to the type of tonality and inflection you naturally bring to them. Imagine being a student in front of their peers and being spoken to in each style. Which way would you prefer? Which style would be most likely to help you get back on track?

The interesting thing is also that the language patterns remain the same when students get it right. It is a simple matter to give praise and feedback using the same words.

> *'I'm delighted to see everybody's keeping safety in mind setting up this experiment.'*
> *'I'm impressed by the way you've chosen to set this out, Mike.'*

Or even add some fun:

> *'I hold you totally responsible for this excellent work Shaqib. It's all your fault that it is a fantastic job!'*

The reality is that if you use a particular set of words, the students will come to associate them with the concepts they represent. The more you use them – the more they associate. Obviously as teachers we will need to explain the ideas and supportive principles behind the 4Rs but this is best done when students have got used to the ideas at a linguistic level.

There are many reasons why this framework is so potent and influential and we offer some of them below. However, we recommend without reservation that you find out for yourself and begin to try out the language patterns and the ideas described here.

The 4Rs framework allows you to become even more influential because:

1. It is fair, equitable and based on common ground.
2. It holds people accountable for the choices they make about their behaviours.

3. It is based around choice rather than coercion and as such goes way beyond the ineffective *'because I say so'* approach.
4. It actually gives you things to say that are redirective without being confrontational.
5. It sets a mutually supportive agenda and then brings it alive through day-to-day language, which keeps it in the front of students' experiences.
6. It offers a framework for catching students doing the right thing.
7. It offers a framework for correcting students when necessary and protects dignity and self-esteem.

As we explore the remaining seven principles, you will see how they are inevitably connected back into the 4Rs framework. In fact, we believe that when you choose to manage your classrooms and engage in your relationships with students through the framework, you naturally and effortlessly encompass all nine core principles automatically.

Look back now to the list on pages 41–2 of the nine core principles. Consider, within your own context and experience, how working within the 4Rs framework will allow you to embrace the other eight principles.

For example, how would it build trust and rapport with your students?

As you explore your ideas, make a note for yourself of any queries, questions or confusions.

If by the time you have finished reading this book you haven't answered those questions to your satisfaction, you could choose to email them to us at the address given at the front of the book.

We *will* reply!

This is far from being an original idea and yet it is common around schools everywhere to hear interactions between teachers and students, which 'fix' a problem or behaviour very firmly within the personality, pathology or identity of the student. Comments that attribute an inappropriate or poor choice of behaviour to some inherent deficiency in the student will almost certainly have one or more of the following effects:

- A reduction or dilution of self-esteem
- An increase in emotional arousal
- Provide corroboration of a negative self-belief
- Erode the relationship between teacher and student
- Most importantly of all, directly inhibit the student's ability to gain a sense of belonging in a socially appropriate way.

The long-term effect of this type of comment is dependent on far too many factors over which the teacher has little control to run the risk of making them in the first place.

Separate the (inappropriate) behaviour from the child

Further, if these sorts of comment are a common experience for students then there is little or no likelihood that they will take the risk of acting differently or making positive changes. It is certainly true that children live down to our expectations.

The reason the word 'inappropriate' is in brackets is to indicate that the opposite is also true. In other words, when students make good choices, it is vital that we reflect these back to them as somehow an inherent part of their character. Phrases (used in age-appropriate ways) such as:

> *'Seeing you include Aaron in the group tells me you are sensitive to others' feelings. That's a great skill.'*
> *'In my experience, other successful learners approach their work with a similar attitude'*

will directly support the sense of belonging that will contribute towards more socially appropriate behaviours.

Use the language of choice

As you will have read above, the language of choice is a significant element in your influential management of students. Of course, it is valuable because it provides a uniquely powerful way of using language. However, its impact goes far deeper than the overt use of language.

A significant majority of behavioural transactions that contain or lead to conflict, result from struggles over relative power. One of the primary features of the language of choice is its recognition that power is essentially the ability to determine outcomes for oneself (see Adler's democratic principles in Chapter 5). Offering real choice is recognition of the power of an individual student to choose what happens next. Of course, within an organisation, there are boundaries and we cannot be talking about a totally free choice. However, a semblance of choice is crucial in supporting empowerment.

It is our experience that at the point one is able to accept intellectually and emotionally, to genuinely embrace the concept of people choosing their own behaviours, conflict disappears. In essence, choice provides the characteristic difference between the polarity thinking between control and management. We have made the point earlier that effective teachers *influence* rather than *control* the behaviour of their students. It is the recognition that students will make a choice anyway and our role is to influence that choice through our use of consequences.

Professor Eric Jensen (1995), one of the world's leading authorities on effective learning, describes 'hope' as one of the primary motivational forces. We agree entirely and find that the language of choice comfortably and pragmatically supports the ideal of hope.

This links closely with the previous principle because when you deal with or address the inappropriate choices a student may make as if they are merely a choice – that is an act separate from personality or character – you model the possibility of real hope and optimism. If it is merely a choice, then next time a similar situation arises the student can make a different and hopefully more valuable choice.

Primary as opposed to secondary behaviours are so called because they represent the sequence in which the behaviours occur. Primary behaviours are those issues that you feel the need to comment on when they begin to infringe mutual rights. They encompass a wide range of behaviours that are usually low level but often high frequency such as talking out of turn, moving around the room without permission or (valid educational) purpose, and behaviours that infringe or hinder the work of other students.

It is when you comment or redirect these students back on task that the secondary behaviours become apparent. Can there be a teacher in the land who hasn't been faced with an, *'It wasn't me!'* when correcting a student we have *seen with our own eyes* throwing litter on the floor?

What, you may ask yourself, is the purpose in denying something that was so blatant? In understanding this, we hit on the core feature of secondary behaviours. Quite simply the response from students is designed to deflect or divert attention from themselves for having been 'caught out' – especially if this occurs in public. There is no real logic or even rational explanation for the things said as secondary behaviours. Provided they protect the fragile self-esteem, they work.

It seems bizarre in the extreme that students are happy to take the flak that these seemingly provocative comments often bring. Especially when the response from adults is often more irritated!

However, as you calmly consider this as an idea that you have encountered frequently, it becomes apparent, does it not, that it takes two to allow events to be sidetracked? When you 'buy in' to these often preposterous secondary behaviours, it is important to recognise that the students are actually dictating the agenda. They are in fact managing your behaviour rather than the other way around.

Think now about some of your more recent experiences of getting dragged into these emotional and linguistic 'culs-de-sac'. How much clearer now is the motive? How uncomfortable do you feel about the way your good intentions are sidetracked without you having been aware of it? When we are 'suckered', who is holding the balance of influence?

In summary, it is important to maintain *our* options for influencing the situation. To do this it becomes necessary to:

- Stay focused on primary behaviours
- Address primary behaviours with minimum fuss and emotional 'heat'
- Reclaim the flow of the lesson as quickly and calmly as possible
- Preserve the student's dignity.

We recommend briefly returning to Chapter 3 at this point and rereading the section on using agreement frames and in particular, *'maybe . . . and . . .'*.

A short while ago we spoke at a conference for all the NQTs within an LEA – approximately 200 recently trained teachers. We asked them how many of them have been given, in some form or another, the following advice:

Keep the focus on primary behaviours

Actively build trust and rapport

'Don't smile until Christmas!'

It was disappointing but no surprise to us when around 90 per cent indicated that they had received this advice. We believe with a passion that this is potentially the most *useless* piece of advice ever given to teachers. Consider the implications of any other work place where the newcomer deliberately refused to smile at any co-workers for three months.

Smiling, being friendly, building suitable positive relationships with students is not in the least incompatible with setting boundaries, saying 'no', or using appropriate sanctions in response to inappropriate behaviours. In fact, the two ideas actually complement each other.

Building rapport is not a question of being someone's best friend. Students want teachers to be friendly but not a friend. In every survey we have encountered that asks students to describe their favourite teacher, the prime qualities alluded to are those of a caring, friendly, fair and firm person. Someone who:

- will listen
- shows interest in you as a person
- gives you a chance
- does not hold grudges
- helps you if you are in difficulties.

Our belief is that the most influential resource you have is you. Building rapport requires genuineness and sincerity, not acting tough by creating an artificial emotional divide between you and your students. Of course, in human relationships establishing balance is the key. Remember our maxim, *'You can't influence anyone from an emotional distance.'*

- We recommend you think of teachers whom you held in high esteem.
- What was it about them that engaged you?
- How did they go about creating that sense of respect you held for them?
- What sorts of things do you imagine they believed about you?
- How did they react to the mistakes you made? Did they ignore them or did they move you back on track in a way that left you feeling supported?
- Pay attention to some of the students and classes with whom you get on particularly well. What are your thoughts and behaviours as you work with them?

The issue of trust is crucial in forming positive and empowering relationships. However, just because you care, just because you are pleasant and friendly, doesn't automatically mean students will trust you. Many students come to school with a fairly well established 'trust deficit'. Their experiences of life have allowed them to learn that adults are not trustworthy. In fact, they break promises, let you down and hurt you. It becomes a considerable risk therefore to invest trust in a teacher just because you appear to be friendly.

Building trust takes time and requires primarily that you act in a trustworthy way. With your students, provide examples that counter their initial lack of trust so that gradually over time the evidence that you provide will oppose their belief that adults cannot be trusted and will help develop the belief that *some* adults can be trusted. Here are some examples:

- Keep promises that you make.
- Pay attention to small personal details – opening doors for them, using please and thank you, etc.
- Treat their poor behaviour as only a choice.
- Treat their good behaviour as a characteristic.
- Apologise when you are wrong or react inappropriately.
- Catch them being good far more frequently than you catch them getting it wrong.
- Find out and show *genuine* interest in their lives and experiences.

We recommend you keep this list in your planner and add to it as new ideas come to you.

> *Treat a man as he is and he will remain as he is. Treat a man as he can and should be and he will become as he can and should be.*
>
> Goethe

Model the behaviour you wish to see

In many ways this is a very self-evident statement. However, as a teacher you are required to manage many different agendas simultaneously in a room that is probably not that well designed or equipped – modelling is sometimes more than a little difficult.

The encouraging thing about modelling is that it is not synonymous with perfection. The fact that you were a human being before you became a teacher buys you certain latitude!

What is important about the concept of modelling is that the positive actions, the respectful language and treatment you offer your students is a *characteristic* of your style. When you get things wrong or lose the plot from time to time, students are quick to forgive provided that their main experiences of you are positive. Further, an appropriate acknowledgement of a mistake, even if that involves an apology, gives you the opportunity to model conflict resolution anyway.

Always follow up on issues that count

The emphasis here is 'issues that count'. Many teachers feel that they have to be manically vigilant and spot every transaction that occurs. This, in part, is sustained by the completely false 'catastrophic thinking' approach that encourages your internal voice to say:

> *'If I let one of them get away with it, they'll ALL do it.'*

The issues that count are essentially those protected by the 4Rs and until you build the sensory experience to make clear decisions about what is and what isn't an appropriate point to intervene, we recommend you be guided by the 4Rs and, in particular, decisions based upon rights infringement.

Of course, you will need to distinguish between managing the day-to-day events of the classroom at the time, and the idea of following up. Following up usually involves further involvement between yourself and the student for some or all of these reasons:

- They have chosen a sanction that involves following up.
- You are concerned that the characteristic response of the student to you is becoming a negative pattern.
- You have deliberately decided to address issues away from the audience.
- You have deliberately given time for emotional arousal (yours or theirs) to dilute before addressing the problem.

We offer some clear strategies and protocols for following up with students in Chapter 6.

Work to repair and restore relationships

It is hopefully abundantly clear from reading this and our other books that we feel that positive relationships are the key to all influence. However, although most teachers fully endorse this as vital good practice, there are specific occasions when some (often unwittingly) disassociate themselves from this idea.

When we correct or redirect students' behaviour or when we apply a sanction, there is always the possibility for a relationship to 'wobble'. The pace and multidimensional aspect of a classroom will mean that, on occasions, we say and do things that have the potential to dent a student's self-esteem.

As neither of these are desirable outcomes that support a healthy and positive classroom climate, it becomes crucial that we are *proactive* in repairing any potential damage. We believe it is a professional responsibility for teachers to do this. The reasons, we hope, are obvious:

- We are the experienced adults.
- We are trained and paid to develop effective learning conditions.
- We are socially more adept and experienced than children.
- If we don't do it, it probably won't happen.

The repairing of a relationship of the nature to which we are referring rarely requires anything major to be done. There is no need to go over the top and lavish praise and attention on the student, for example. More often than not, it is a simple word or gesture that lets the student know that we have moved on and that we still care. Imagine a student who has moved to sit on their own as a result of the sanction you applied in response to their poor choice. Moving to the student a few minutes later and saying simply:

'How are you getting on? Do you need a hand?'

is sufficient to reconnect and let them know that even though you will follow through with their choices, you will not hold a grudge.

If you do not offer them a way back with dignity, then bit by bit you are throwing away your ability to influence what goes on with them in your classroom, so it seems to us a valuable investment.

Questions for professional development

What do you feel about the topics covered in this chapter?

What are some of the implications of the topics within your classroom?

What do you think is the most important for you to remember from this chapter?

Chapter 5

Purposeful behaviour

A child needs encouragement like a plant needs sun and water. Unfortunately those who need encouragement most, get it the least because they behave in such a way that our reaction to them pushes them further into discouragement and rebellion.

Rudolf Dreikurs

Something within each of us cries out for belonging. We can have all the world has to offer in terms of status, achievement and possessions, yet without a true sense of belonging, our lives feel empty and pointless.

John O'Donohue

Students who present difficult and challenging behaviour present one of the major obstacles to teacher effectiveness in the classroom. They can cause us to feel disempowered and dejected. They can cause us to feel hopeless or angry, anxious or enraged. They can cause us to give up on some of the most vulnerable students in our classrooms and begin to introduce stricter and harsher strategies in order to regain some feeling of control. Some may even cause us to reject them totally via permanent exclusion. (The reasons for this 'emotional hijacking' are examined in Chapter 6.) If these students were not so potentially destructive to our ability to teach them, we wouldn't give them such significance. To counter this, DeBruyn (1983) suggests that if some teachers spent as much time trying to understand the reasons behind a student's behaviour as they do trying to control it through sanctions and punishments then far more discipline problems would be resolved. In this chapter it is our intention to help you become even more influential through both an understanding of some of the major, underlying causes of misbehaviour and some of the frameworks of support that you can put in place.

Alfred Adler (cited in Mosak 1999) proposed what he called his five 'democratic principles'. In very brief summary, these are:

Democratic principles

Man is a social being

Man's main desire is to belong. This need for a true sense of belonging is one of our most powerful desires beyond the need for survival. An understanding of how fundamental a need for belonging is will form the basis for your understanding of most of the difficult behaviours you will meet in the classroom. This understanding will enable you to become even more influential with those students you frequently find the hardest to reach.

All behaviour is purposeful

The second of Adler's democratic principles suggests that we cannot understand the behaviour of another person unless we can understand its purpose – the goal to which it is directed. He goes on to suggest that the goal is *always* to find a way of moving towards a sense of personal significance or belonging.

Man is a decision-making organism

Next, Adler suggests that we *decide* what we want to do both at a conscious and unconscious level. We are not the victims of outside forces such as heredity and environment. These certainly can provide the setting factors within which we make our choices but ultimately we choose our own behaviour. It is this notion that allows us to be optimistic in our behaviour towards children. It is within this democratic principle that you find the roots of the highly influential and supportive technique that we termed, in *Confident Classroom Leadership* (Hook and Vass 2000a), the 'language of choice'.

Man is a whole being

Man is greater than the sum of his parts. Simply gathering information about the various background factors in a student's life does not mean we will have a useful explanatory model of the student's current behaviour. We cannot understand students through understanding what must necessarily always be a set of partial characteristics. We must work on, and support, changes in resulting patterns of behaviour rather than always trying to have a detailed, explanatory model before we take action. Just because Suzy comes from a broken home, her mother was a heroin addict, she missed a considerable amount of schooling in Key Stage 1, she has asthma and her stepmother is a magistrate doesn't mean that you have a complete, explanatory model of Suzy's current behaviour. Nor does it mean that you cannot provide effective support for Suzy. The understanding we have of Suzy's background is just part of the complexity that is Suzy and we must never see it as more than this. Nevertheless, by understanding Suzy's current, presenting patterns of behaviour we can bring our skills and influence to bear to work on helping Suzy develop more effective patterns of behaviour that will, in return, enable her to gain a greater sense of belonging in school.

This is not to deny that an understanding of the context within which students function is not often very useful, sometimes crucial to our ability to become influential with those students. Rather, it suggests that we can frequently be highly influential without the necessity for detailed problem analysis.

Man does not see reality as it is

We 'understand' reality only so far as we perceive it. This perception may be mistaken or biased. If we are to influence and support students in making more socially acceptable choices about their behaviour then we must help them change their perception of their current circumstances. Equally, we may need to change the way in which we perceive the students' behaviour in order to open up new possibilities for change. We have frequently experienced a situation in which some teachers have described a student's behaviour as 'impossible' while others see it as 'difficult but manageable. He has his ups and downs.' We'll leave you to guess which teachers are likely to be more successful in providing support to the student.

It is the very fact that all behaviour is purposeful that means the 'one-size-fits-all' approach to discipline that many teachers – and schools – adopt is so ineffective in influencing those students whose behaviour does not fit within the broad band of 'socially acceptable' behaviours that the majority of students use to gain a sense of belonging.

Neil

It doesn't seem to matter what you do, Neil is constantly interrupting and calling attention to himself. When you had him sat at the front you kept finding yourself drawn into unnecessary and inconsequential conversations. When you moved him to the back of the room, his hand is constantly waving in the air making unnecessary requests or offering 'off the wall' answers to your questions. If you try ignoring his behaviour he starts to provoke other students, forcing you to intervene. At times he seems too good to be true and you find yourself drawn to give him lots of attention to try and reinforce these good moments. At the end of a session with Neil, you feel frustrated and drained of energy. If only he would just sit down and get on with his work like the rest!

Jarrell

Jarrell is very different. He is always the last to arrive and, when he does decide to grace your classroom with his presence, his entrance is always dramatic. When you ask him to sit down and get on with some work, everything about his expression and body language screams at you, '*You are going to get me to do that how!?*' The other day you gave him the choice of completing his work in the lesson or staying in at lunch-time to complete it. Jarrell's reply was simply to refuse to do the work and when you asked him to stay behind he looked straight at you and said, '*You can't make me stay! I'm going*' and he walked off. If you confront his behaviour, he seems to revel in the challenge. Several times you have felt so threatened by his confrontational behaviours that you have resorted to, '*I've had enough of this behaviour. Get out of my room!*'

Fara

The other day things went missing from your handbag. Your money wasn't touched but the photographs of your children and your car keys went missing. You are sure that Fara was to blame but you can't prove it. Fara seems to delight in making herself unpopular. She falsely and blatantly accuses others of acts they have not committed. She says hurtful things and regularly spoils their work. There have been many complaints from parents that Fara is bullying younger and more vulnerable children on the playground. It doesn't seem to matter how often you remind yourself that students like Fara need your care more than any other, you find her almost impossible to like and you long for the days when she doesn't come to school.

Kyle

When you think of Kyle you find yourself shaking your head in exasperation. You've tried everything you know to be supportive and yet the work still isn't being done. The only time Kyle produces any work is when you are sitting beside him and he stops as soon as you move away. Whenever you see him about the school he is on his own or on the periphery of groups watching but not joining in. He is frequently absent from school with minor illnesses and you are convinced that he is taking lots of unnecessary time off school. At times he seems to live in a fantasy world and at other times the best you can say is that he is there in body but not in spirit. You would dearly like to help him, and you know he could be successful but part of you also knows he is a hopeless case.

The student who is constantly calling out at inappropriate times does not necessarily have the same goal as the student who constantly challenges and confronts the teacher. Equally, the student who is constantly late to lessons may well be operating from within a very different motivational framework than the class bully. Influential teachers, by understanding the fundamental human 'longing to belong' and the way in which an inability to gain a socially appropriate sense of belonging will create a different motivational force behind a student's choices, can begin to target their skills and resources and tune their own emotional response to work to support students in achieving their motivational goals in more socially appropriate ways.

Another of the keys to becoming even more influential in your classroom is to begin to understand these motivational purposes behind student behaviour.

It would be simplistic in the extreme to suggest that all behavioural difficulties can be attributed to just four primary motivational purposes. Nevertheless, the vast majority of behavioural difficulties teachers encounter, both within their classrooms and around schools, have their origins in four key, primary purposes for gaining a sense of belonging. Many students use these goals when they find themselves unable to gain this crucial sense of belonging in more socially appropriate ways. These primary, but inappropriate purposes are:

- the need for attention
- the gaining of power
- the need for revenge and
- the defence of self-confidence.

The ways in which students go about attaining these purposes can lead to the sorts of behaviours that leave you experiencing feelings of frustration, anger, annoyance and helplessness – to name just a few.

It therefore makes sense to accept that, if we can understand these purposes, and if we can help students gain a sense of belonging in more socially appropriate ways we can significantly increase our influence within the classroom. We cannot become more influential if we do not have some models within which to exert this influence. It is for this reason that we believe it is important to examine one of the most influential models of student behaviour proposed in the twentieth century – that of the eminent American child psychiatrist Rudolf Dreikurs.

Dreikurs, basing his work upon Adler's democratic principles, proposed that the prime goal of a student's behaviour in a classroom is to achieve a sense of recognition and belonging. Many students achieve this sense of recognition and belonging in what teachers would view as socially acceptable ways. They complete their work, they operate in cooperative groups, they take responsibility, etc. In other words, they have learned a set of interpersonal skills that will enable them to achieve social acceptability within our classrooms. Some children, for a variety of reasons, do not have the skill set necessary to achieve recognition and belonging within our classrooms in such an acceptable way. Nevertheless, they are driven by this prime human need of belonging (what John O'Donohue (2000) calls the human 'longing to belong') and, in order to get at least a temporary sense of recognition, they will attempt to achieve their goals through one (or more) of the inappropriate, but purposeful, behaviours mentioned above. Students can attempt to achieve these four key purposes via a range of strategies that can (with the exception of the protection of self-confidence) take both a passive and active form. Figure 5.1 sets out some of these

Purpose	Active	Teacher Response	Passive	Teacher Response
Gaining attention Gets attention – temporary cessation of behaviour – behaviour begins again	Showing off Class clown Embarrassing behaviours A nuisance Calling out Tapping etc. 'Winding-up' others	Annoyance Frustration 'It doesn't matter what I do, five minutes later . . .!' Irritation	Shy Constant need for support Lethargy Overly anxious Too cute to be true The 'model' pupil	Feeling the need to coax Flattered by their attention Unnecessary giving of support
Gaining power Gets attention – behaviour continues or increases	Argumentative Openly defiant Truants from lessons Bullying Temper tantrums 'You can't make me . . .' Lying	'Let's see who is the boss!' Anger Threatened Need to win 'How dare you!'	Stubborn Laziness Forgetfulness Passive resistance Uncooperative	Exasperation Frustration Victory when student complies
Gaining revenge Gets attention – switches to more extreme behaviours	Vicious Cruel to peers Destruction of others' property Spiteful Gang leader	Hurt Under seige 'Why is he doing this to me?'	Sullen Moody Defiant Miserable	'If that's the way you want it . . .' Feels the pupil is unthankful
Protecting self-confidence Gets attention – remains uncooperative or passive	Not applicable	Not applicable	Babyish behaviour Fantasises Hopelessness Solitary Resistance to support Situational avoidance	Helplessness Exasperation Lowered expectations

Figure 5.1 How students attempt to achieve their goals

ways that students might attempt to attain these purposes together with some of the feelings these behaviours can elicit in teachers.

Attention seeking, in itself, is not a disruptive behaviour. When done well it is a highly desirable yet complex set of subtle, interpersonal micro-skills that require the person utilising them to be very sensitive to the body language signals and intonation patterns given out by those whose attention they are trying to seek. Most of your interactions with others would not be possible if you were unable to gain their positive attention. It is this attention that, in return, is a major contributor towards your sense of self-worth – *'others recognise and attend to me'* – and identity – *'I am someone who is valued and worthy of the attention of others.'*

It is perhaps because this skill is both so fundamental to human communication and the sense of self-worth and identity and yet requires such a complex set of social skills to carry it out in a socially acceptable manner that so many children find it difficult to attain the sense of social recognition that will enable them to be successful in the complexity of a classroom or school situation.

Those students who, for whatever reason, have not developed the complex set of skills necessary to enable them to gain the attention of others in a socially appropriate way will resort to other, less appropriate, attention-gaining strategies. These are the students who speak out of turn, arrive deliberately late to class, constantly tap on the desk in an irritating fashion and make strange noises all of which are designed to force your attention. Some of these students will even tell us of the troubles they have caused and the bad things they have done. All of these attention-gaining misbehaviours – and the 1,001 others that we are sure you can add to the list – are all designed to achieve one purpose – your undivided attention.

If these students cannot gain your attention in appropriate ways they will misbehave to get their purpose met. If you ignore their inappropriate attention-gaining strategies, they will escalate the situation – 'I will _make_ you give me attention.' If we react to their behaviour we feed their need – negative attention is better than no attention at all. The problem these students have is that our reaction to their behaviour is not good emotional 'food'. It lasts only a few minutes and the hunger for attention returns. These are the students who can frequently bring forth the well-known teacher's phrase, *'It doesn't matter what I say or do – five minutes later she's at it again!'* Of course she does. Every time she seeks attention she gets a reaction from the teacher and so the cycle continues.

It is the frequency as much, if not more than, the intensity of this inappropriate attention-gaining behaviour that caused it to be described in the Elton Report (1989) as 'making it harder for teachers to teach and pupils to learn'.

> **Scan the 'Gaining attention' row of Figure 5.1 then think through the students you teach. List those of them who seem to have behaviours that are designed to gain your attention by misbehaving.**

Primary Purpose 2 – Gaining power

Again, this is not abnormal human behaviour. Understanding about dominance and position are necessary to be able to function appropriately within our society. Young children will experiment with their behaviour in order to establish their position and level of dominance over the adults in their lives. We are sure you have all seen (or experienced at first hand if you have had young children of your own) young children who adopt the 'Violet Elizabeth' approach to human interactions – '*I will scream, and scream and scream until Mummy buys me a bar of chocolate.*' Fortunately for us, the vast majority of these children come to understand that there are certain clearly established boundaries in adult–child relationships and they come to learn more appropriate ways of belonging with the adults in their lives other than through dominance.

Dreikurs (1974: 36) suggests, 'If parents and teachers do not employ correct methods to stop the demand for undue attention, the child becomes a power-seeker.' The child begins to develop 'faulty logic' that says, '*If you don't let me do what I want, you don't love me*' or '*I only belong when you do what I want you to do.*'

Some of these students will argue, lie, constantly contradict, refuse cooperation, deliberately commit unacceptable acts and be openly disobedient. Others will become stubborn, openly lazy or passively disobedient (see Figure 5.1). Most teachers' 'normal' response to these behaviours is to feel threatened. In particular, they feel that their ability to lead the class is undermined. In an attempt to regain a sense of control these teachers will, themselves, resort to power-seeking behaviours of their own. They will return the power struggle – '*I'll show you who's boss!*' These efforts to meet a power struggle by returning the struggle are *always* ineffective for the simple reason that the students involved are not really interested in the outcome. It is the power struggle itself that feeds their longing to belong.

> Scan the 'Gaining power' row of Figure 5.1 then think through the students you teach. List those of them who seem to have behaviours that are designed to gain power by misbehaving.

Primary Purpose 3 – Gaining revenge

If children feel so put down by those around them (other children *and* adults) they will move from power seeking towards seeking retaliation. Some children only feel that they have a sense of self-worth when they have made others hurt as badly as they do. However, this need for revenge is not confined simply to those students who are the most damaged – we are all capable of resorting to this behaviour when we feel hurt by others. Teachers who send a child out of their class to be 'punished' by a more senior member of staff are often engaging in revenge-seeking behaviours. They will not be satisfied if the student is simply, calmly and rationally talked to by the senior member of staff (despite this being the most likely form of resolution), they want retribution – '*He has hurt me and I will settle for nothing less than seeing him hurt in return.*' By resorting to this more primitive need for revenge, some teachers bring out the worst side of their behaviour.

These students see life as grossly unfair and, because they are convinced that all those who surround them hopelessly dislike them, they set out to respond in kind – *'Get your retaliation in first!'* These students have a deep distrust of teachers and, because they can be quite ruthless in pursuing their goal of revenge, they are among the most difficult students to like. Their actions can often be violent, vicious and brutal. If they are defeated in their attempts for revenge, they will often come back with even more extreme behaviours.

Dreikurs (1974: 39) suggests that the leaders of juvenile gangs are often seeking revenge:

> *'They see the whole of society as their enemy and frequently look down on others with contempt. Yet underneath the façade they are deeply discouraged individuals with little hope for themselves.'*

Those students who engage in this sort of behaviour at a high level of frequency are among the hardest to work with in the mainstream sector. Many of them will need professional help beyond the classroom. Punishment and sanction will frequently serve to confirm their negative view of themselves. Positive consequences are only effective if the students care about themselves. Fortunately, students who are hurting inside so badly that revenge seeking comprises their most frequent set of classroom behaviours are rare. While we have included some possible strategies (below) that you can consider using to support these students, these are most appropriate for those students who only display this sort of behaviour from time to time. If a student is regularly engaging in these behaviours, alongside the support you provide for the student in class, we would strongly suggest that you seek the support of other colleagues in and possibly beyond school.

Scan the 'Gaining revenge' row of Figure 5.1 then think through the students you teach. List those of them who seem to have behaviours that are designed to gain revenge.

For some students the world becomes an emotionally hostile place. Their self-image is so poor that they will set out to protect what little sense of self-worth they have left. These students will withdraw from any challenge they are faced with. They adopt the simple protection technique of 'If I'm not in the race then I can't lose.' This can be withdrawal from both academic and social behaviour. Some of these students will have arrived at this point after unsuccessfully trying to gain a sense of belonging through attention gaining, power struggling and revenge seeking. Others at an early age come to the conclusion that they are not as capable as others and have no chance of becoming loveable and capable.

As long as these students can protect themselves from exposure to the potential of failure, they can at least present the illusion of belonging to the group. This behaviour may be generalised across the student's entire world or it may be specific to those areas in which the

Primary Purpose 4 – Protection of self-confidence

student feels most vulnerable. Whichever it is, it can frequently be quite contagious and cause teachers to give up in exasperation.

> *It is very difficult for the teacher not to fall for the child's provocation that 'You can't do anything with me so leave me alone.' The natural reaction is for the teacher to give up.*

(Dreikurs 1974: 39)

Scan the 'Protecting self-confidence' row of Figure 5.1 then think through the students you teach. List those of them who seem to have behaviours that are designed to protect their self-confidence.

Possible influential frameworks

Establishing the purpose

Dreikurs suggests that the first step in managing all of these behaviours is to openly confront it by confirming and disclosing the purpose to the student. This disclosure should be done without criticism or attempts to dominate. It is best to adopt a note of curiosity rather than criticism – *'Could it be that . . . ?'* rather than *'What you are doing is . . .'*

Dreikurs suggests the following conversational structure that can be used in post-lesson discussions or can be modified to become part of a quiet, private word in class:

Teacher: *'Do you know why you . . . ?'*
Student: *'No'* (they probably genuinely don't know at a conscious level).
Teacher: *'I've got a few ideas. Would you mind if I shared them with you?'*
Student: *'Alright'* (in our experience they rarely refuse).
Teacher: (In a non-judgemental way asks the following questions one at a time to allow for the 'recognition reflex' – see below)
   a. *'Could it be that you want me to give you special attention or that you want me to notice you?'*
   b. *'Could it be that you want to be the boss in the classroom or that you want to show me that nobody can make you do things?'*
   c. *'Could it be that you want to hurt other students (or me) as much as you think they are hurting you?'*
   d. *'Could it be that you want us all to leave you alone?'*

Rarely if ever will you get a verbal 'Yes' to any of these questions. Rather, you will notice the signs of a recognition reflex that might be a little smile, a raising of the eyebrows, a slight nod, etc. In other words, while the mouth might be saying 'No', the body language is saying 'Yes. That's right.' Even if you notice the signs of recognition at your first question, it is worth continuing with the other three as some students will be attempting to achieve more than one purpose depending upon the circumstances in which they find themselves.

Once you have a reasonably good idea of the likely purpose behind the behaviour, the following sections will provide you with a framework within which you can build influential strategies to support the students. However, when utilising any of these frameworks you must always remember that most of these students do not have the skill set necessary to enable them to gain a sense of belonging in a socially appropriate way. Therefore, simple strategies such as increasing praise will not, by themselves, be successful until you have taught the student new skills. This teaching process need not be lengthy and complicated. It is often sufficient to simply suggest a more appropriate response and then play 'catch them using the new skill'.

Teacher: *'Jonathan, what I need you to choose to do is to go back to your seat and sit down'* (pause to allow Jonathan to make a good choice – after Jonathan has sat down) *'Thanks. I appreciate that, Jonathan.'*

The following frameworks – combined with those strategies outlined in Chapter 3, which are designed to proactively teach skills – will give you an influential context that you will probably have to adapt to both fit with the age of student you are supporting and your preferred, positive intervention strategies.

A framework of influence for 'gaining attention'

You can't ignore the attention-seeking behaviour. If you try, the student may well simply escalate their attempts – 'I will _make_ you give me attention!'

- Your first strategy must be to establish a simple way of giving minimal attention for the inappropriate behaviour. This may simply be the use of a quick phrase – *'Neil, I've noticed that'* – or rapid gesture – the blocking hand and brief nod.
- Next you must briefly teach appropriate behaviour: *'Neil, when I see you on task, working independently, then I will know you are saying to yourself "I can cope without constantly asking for my teacher's attention."'*
- Now you need to put *yourself* on a behaviour modification programme. Make sure that you intervene with positive attention whenever you notice the student engaging in socially acceptable behaviours – particularly the targeted behaviour. Remember: Whatever behaviour gets your maximum attention will increase.

A framework of influence for 'gaining power'

You cannot win a power struggle with a power struggler, therefore your best plan is to avoid the confrontation. You can achieve this in several ways. However, the most effective framework is:

- Begin by accepting three simple truths:
  - You do have a right to teach.
  - Your students – all of them – do have a right to learn.
  - You do not have a right to *make* students learn.
- Recognise that resisting a student who wants a power struggle is not easy. You will have to prepare yourself in advance. Working out a 'script' that you can fall back on can be a very successful strategy:
  - *'I'm sorry that you feel upset* (validate to enhance agreement), *but I cannot allow you to carry on with this behaviour as it is stopping us all learning. If you continue to choose* (behaviour) *then you will be choosing* (consequence).'
  - *'Yes, I agree that you might think it is unfair, but if you choose to continue* (behaviour) *you will be choosing* (consequence).'
  - You might even agree with the student – *'You're right, I can't make you, but if you choose not to then you will be choosing* (consequence).'

    It is difficult to fight with a teacher who has just agreed with your position!
- Remind the student of the fair, agreed 4Rs Framework (Chapter 4):
  - *'Jarrell, remember that we all agreed that everybody has the right to learn and I have a right to teach? Are you going back on that agreement? Can you suggest a way in which we can all enjoy our rights and you can still feel good?'* (Be prepared to suggest a couple of ways when Jarrell says 'No'. Remember, you must actively teach Jarrell how to belong in a socially acceptable way.)
- As soon as Jarrell stops the behaviour and you can return to teaching, remember to thank him – *'Thanks for making a good choice, Jarrell. I appreciate that.'*
- Many power-seeking students find direct, public praise hard to accept. However, experience shows that if you put a delay between the student's good choice and your positive feedback it will be more effective. Therefore, rather than using the sort of intense 'catch him being good' strategy that you would employ for attention-seeking, notice the student's good choice and then a short while later use more private praise such as a quiet *'Thanks for that Jarrell. I appreciated the effort you were making just then'* or a simple smile, nod and thumbs up.
- One other strategy that sometimes works with power-seeking behaviour is to do the opposite of what the student expects:

  If Jarrell is drumming away with his pencil while the teacher is trying to introduce the next part of her music lesson, she might choose to say something like, *'Jarrell, would you like to sit next to me and have these drumsticks then you can help me set the rhythm for the rest of the class?'*

  Charlene is obviously starting to become more challenging in her behaviour and, as the teacher walks past her desk, Charlene turns to her work partner and says in a stage whisper, *'I don't see why we should do this boring crap anyway.'* The teacher might turn back for a second and say something like, *'I'm sorry, you're right, this bit is a bit boring, isn't it Charlene? Never mind, I'm sure you'll see why we needed to do it when we move on to the next section. Would you like me to give you a hand so we can finish it a bit quicker?'*

These strategies are designed to take your sail out of the student's wind.

A framework of influence for 'gaining revenge'

As we said above, revenge seekers are among the hardest students to support within a classroom for the simple reason that they have little regard for what happens to them. In fact, any attempt to suppress or dominate their behaviour will simply fuel their belief that the world is set on hurting them.

You might find that some students are so committed to hurting you that you have to seek the support of others both within (e.g. the SENCO) and beyond (e.g. the Educational Psychologist) your school. However, we have often found that the following framework can be helpful:

- Actively set out to notice any times when these students utilise socially acceptable strategies for gaining recognition from either yourself or their peers. Once you have found some of these times, point them out to the revenge seekers and, when they occur again, use low-level recognition – smile, nods, etc. – to spotlight and reinforce them.
- If possible, enlist the support of key, socially able students in supportive work groups that involve your targeted students – teach them that they are likeable.
- Whatever you do, do not show them or tell them that they have hurt you.
- Formal sanctions hierarchies tend to alienate these students so, in discussion with them, negotiate and utilise logical, natural consequences:
  - *'If you choose not to do the work in lesson, you will be choosing to do it in your own time.'*
  - *'If you choose to throw bricks at other children, you will be choosing not to use the bricks.'*
  - *'If you choose to throw paint down the sink, you will be choosing to clean it up.'*
  - *'If you choose to continually shout out and change the channels while we watch the television, you will be choosing to go to work with Mr Johnson while we continue with the lesson.'*

A framework of influence for 'protection of self-confidence'

Your influence with these students lies in your ability to help them realise and build on their strengths. Components of an influential framework are:

- As with the 'revenge seekers', actively set out to notice any times when these students utilise socially acceptable strategies for gaining recognition from either yourself or their peers. Once you have found some of these times, point them out to the students and, when they occur again, use low-level recognition – smile, nods, etc. – to spotlight and reinforce them.
- Make sure that they can be successful with any work you set them. Don't set them up for academic failure.
- Break work down into small, achievable steps. Say things like, *'Fara, I'd like you to just try the first two of these and then put your hand up and I'll come over to see how you're getting on.'* In this way you will be able to provide much more frequent positive feedback.
- If these students make mistakes, look for opportunities to take the blame yourself – *'I'm sorry Fara, I didn't explain that properly. Let me sit beside you and I'll explain it again.'*
- If they are experiencing unacceptable pressure from parents then you may – possibly with advice from colleagues such as a Key Stage Coordinator, Head of Year, etc. – have to get between the students and their parents and help the parents set more realistic goals for their children. This might mean that, for a while, you will have to use your influence in helping the parents set what, to them, seem to be unnecessarily low expectations for their children while their self-confidence is repaired. Some of the language patterns outlined in other chapters will help you here.
- Enlisting the support of more socially able peers can prove very effective with students who have poor self-confidence. Supportive work groups and cooperative playground groups can bring about rapid changes in classroom behaviour.
- On some occasions, particularly within the primary sectors, it has proved possible to build supportive programmes for some of these students in Key Stage 2 whereby they spend a small amount of each day working as a helper in a class of younger students (Reception or Year 1). Younger students can often provide the sort of unconditional regard that succeeds in rapidly rebuilding self-confidence across a range of areas.

Questions for professional development

What do you feel about the topics covered in this chapter?

What are some of the implications of the topics within your classroom?

What do you think is the most important for you to remember from this chapter?

Chapter 6

Influencing solutions

You'll cop an unfortunate one in a minute, Rodney, so help me!
Derek Trotter – 'Only Fools and Horses'

In this chapter we offer some fundamental insights into the effect of emotional arousal on your ability to access the skills and understanding that you know underpin good practice. In addition, we explore some practical strategies for positively influencing situations that may go beyond the classroom, such as:

- following up after class with a student
- working with conflict and anger.

It may be stating the obvious but one's ability to use the constructive skills and strategies learned and developed throughout one's career to best effect, i.e. to generate positive outcomes that maintain a learning focus and support self-esteem, is significantly enhanced when the teacher is able to remain calm and rational. It is a simple truth that we are able to consider more options, see things from different perspectives, and listen with clarity and understanding when emotional arousal is kept at manageable levels.

   Here we offer a very simplified explanation, based on current neurological research, as to *why* it is essential to manage our own emotional states effectively by *deliberately* cultivating strategies that assist us in remaining as calm and rational as humanly possible. It offers a clear scientific, evidence-based approach against which you can check your own strategies. If you would like to explore these ideas in more detail, we recommend *The APET Model* by Joe Griffin and Ivan Tyrell (2000).

   In Chapter 4 we talked about the 'guts to gob' approach to behaviour management during which we react in an unplanned way to student behaviours and from a more emotionally driven state. We hope you are very clear in your own mind and also in your own practice that this approach is neither valuable nor effective. However, we believe it is of value to have a clear and conscious understanding of why this is so. Several times during this book we have referred to the phrase 'emotional

Emotional arousal

hijacking,' first used by Daniel Goleman in his seminal book *Emotional Intelligence* (1996). Emotional hijacking occurs when emotional arousal becomes too strong and prevents or hijacks clear, logical thinking. Obviously some levels of emotional arousal are vital to keep us safe, motivated, curious, hopeful and so on. However, beyond a certain level, emotional arousal has the effect of making us stupid – literally!

The model

All information entering the brain passes through the limbic system where it is 'analysed' to establish whether it presents a danger or not. This analysis is in the form of matching the incoming information to patterns that exist already in the brain derived from previous experiences. The pattern matching process triggers an instant emotional reaction, allowing the 'fight or flight' response to be triggered in turn as a counter to any potential threat. This is obviously an essential mechanism for survival. All of this occurs at a non-conscious level, i.e. we are unaware it is going on.

The effect of this is to act as a kind of filter for sensory information entering the brain. It is only once this filtering has occurred that information is 'delivered' to the thinking part of the brain – the neocortex. In other words, if the emotional brain *interprets* a situation as being challenging or threatening it remains highly aroused and the information will not therefore be 'delivered' to the neocortex. A key word here is 'interprets'. For example, when faced with a student who challenges or defies instructions, the teacher is not *actually* threatened or in danger in the sense that most confrontations are relatively low level and verbal in nature. However, it is possible in the teacher's brain to 'match' this classroom experience to an (unrealistic) belief that 'good' teachers should be able to *control* students, with the result that emotional arousal will be high because as a result of this inappropriate pattern match, by implication, this particular teacher cannot regard him or herself as 'good'. Equally, it is possible to match to a pattern that has no direct connection with school or work. It is possible to make a metaphorical link between this classroom stand-off and a previous experience where the teacher was embarrassed or felt powerless in a public setting. For example, the classroom experience may 'match' to the time when the teacher 'fluffed' lines during a local dramatic production in front of friends and family. This was a stressful experience too and matching to it will generate a similarly high level of emotional arousal.

This state of high emotional arousal is of necessity a very one-dimensional type of response. If a lion were to walk into your lounge this evening you would be extremely unlikely to consider how it got there or be fascinated by its size and majesty! You would consider only one dimension in responding – to run or hide!

This one-dimensional 'fight or flight' response may manifest back in the classroom as an increase in aggression in the voice and a more confrontational response, *'How dare you speak to me that way! You're in detention!'* However, on stage, the actor may become almost transfixed as his mind remains totally blank and the lines that he knows really well and could rattle off in rehearsal become temporarily lost to him. In other words, this high emotional arousal denies us access to the part of our brain (the neocortex) that allows us to take a more objective viewpoint and consider different perspectives. The teacher loses touch with accepted good practice of responding calmly but assertively and the actor cannot mentally step back to find something he knows well.

Since the neocortex is the part of the brain that provides the fine detail or subtle distinctions of interpretation and brings logic and rational thinking to bear on situations, the implications of this knowledge for your interactions with students and the emotions associated with them are, in our view, profound. Essentially, in simple terms, if stress and tension build to unmanageable levels while managing students' behaviours we will become disconnected from or denied access to the logical knowledge we hold regarding what is good practice.

In our workshops, when we ask colleagues to elicit the differences between a successful and less than satisfactory piece of behaviour management, the ability to stay calm is universally emphasised as being the decisive factor.

Few teachers would argue that the core purpose of a classroom is to enhance learning. We naturally include social and emotional learning as well as intellectual learning. If the simple truth is that under circumstances of high emotional arousal we are unable to have a rational conversation with students and that we become disconnected from the logical knowledge of good practice, then all our strategies both for managing *ourselves and the classroom* should be *deliberately* structured to minimise emotional arousal.

Take this opportunity to think back over the strategies and ideas, the language patterns and the organising principles you have read and thought about. You may choose to flick back over the pages reviewing the ones that were more significant for you – the ones that resonated most, which had a feel to them or with which you were most comfortable.

As you do this, consider them in light of the information above and create a clear sense of how, when you are using them, they will help maintain reasonable levels of emotional arousal.

One of the nine core principles is 'Always follow up on issues that count'. For us, issues that count are certainly those where the basic rights outlined in the 4Rs are infringed in some way. In many cases, the following up will take place within the context of the lesson initially by the way we manage the students' choices and utilise appropriate rewards and sanctions. It will also occur through taking individuals to one side for a quiet and private word to listen to their point of view, restate expectations and redirect them to success.

However, there are occasions when we will need to go further than this and spend some additional time with a student beyond the

Resolving difficulties beyond the classroom

classroom. These situations are valuable for many reasons – for example, as a natural part of your hierarchy of sanctions, to discuss concerns or to complete work. They may also be necessary if you experience a pattern of response from the student, which is not compatible with maintaining a positive relationship, such as frequent sulkiness or repeated secondary behaviours when given instructions in class.

There is an issue of influence at stake in following up with students too. There are times when exiting a student from class to another location is absolutely correct and justified. It is also important to use whatever referral procedures exist in school to inform others of certain behaviours. However, the role of the class teacher does not end there. It is vital that you play some part in the process that follows exit or referral, as they are key emotional and psychological times to restate expectations and to repair the relationship. Both of these tasks provide significant potential for influencing future outcomes.

It is worth remembering that any instruction to remain behind after class or to return at a given time is likely to trigger, at best, some annoyance and irritation on the part of the student. It also has the potential to trigger anxiety, anger and strong resentment. Again, these feelings are the emotional responses resulting from pattern matches to previous experiences. Put simply, they 'know' they are going to 'get done' and they 'know' it will not be a pleasant experience.

Under these circumstances, in order to maximise the opportunities to have a rational and meaningful (in terms of resolution) conversation with the student, to emphasise the key ideas of protecting mutual rights and to connect with any desire or competence to improve things next time, we need to take deliberate steps to ensure emotional arousal is diluted.

As a process for following up that fulfils the criteria above, we recommend the following protocols.

1. Thank the student for staying behind (or returning)

It may seem a strange thing to do but starting with a positive comment serves to put the student at ease. Further, it is a point of success and a good choice the student has made and these are always valuable to emphasise. If you are not convinced yet, how about remembering the simple fact that you haven't got to go chasing the student – they have saved you time and energy! If you begin by praising or thanking the student you are, in effect, making a positive emotional deposit into the emotional account you have with the student before you make the inevitable withdrawal by discussing more difficult issues.

2. Validate and acknowledge their feelings

It is a fair assumption that they will be feeling nervous, aggrieved, inconvenienced or all three! Use the impact of an agreement frame to reduce emotional arousal, validate their perspective and create a point of influence:

'I imagine you're a little annoyed at missing part of break, Steve' ('Too right I am!') *'and it's important that we sort this out and move on.'*

3. Focus on specific, observable behaviours

'This morning I spoke to you four times about calling to Mike across the room'

is more effective and identifiable than

'You were mucking about and disturbing the lesson far too much today.'

It is also less likely to be defended or denied if it is a verifiable and factual observation. If the student attempts a secondary behaviour, *'I wasn't the only one!'* then use the 'maybe ... and ...' approach to refocus.

4. Describe the impact of the behaviour using 'I' messages

'When (they don't always do it) *you call across the room to friends* (description) *I get irritated* (your response) *as I can't focus on helping students and it disturbs concentration* (the effect).'

5. Relate the behaviour and its impact to mutual rights

This reminds the student that a framework binding all of us exists and diminishes the likelihood of the 'what's the big deal?' response. It also moves beyond the 'because I said so' justification:

'We've all agreed that I have a right to teach and you all have a right to learn and when you shout out it makes it difficult for us all to enjoy these rights.'

6. Offer the right of reply

Give the student an opportunity to suggest a motive for their behaviour although keep alert to the idea of secondary behaviours and refer it back to mutual rights if necessary. You may simply ask, 'Is what you were doing against the rules?' The importance of getting the student to identify some motive for the behaviour is that it leads neatly to the next step . . .

7. Consider alternatives

Sometimes the student's motive is, in principle, acceptable but the method of achieving it inappropriate – they wanted to know how to do something and you were busy so they repeatedly shouted out at you. It is always valuable to get the student to suggest how they might meet their goal in more useful ways or at more appropriate times. When you ask them to offer a solution as to what they could do next time this goal occurs, be sure to get them to frame it positively. In other words, we want them to describe exactly what they *will* do that is acceptable rather than what they will *not* do.

> *'I'll wait for you or quietly ask someone closer'* is better than, *'I won't call out any more.'*

8. Emphasise personal responsibility and expectation

Use the language of choice to emphasise accountability and focus on your confidence and expectation that the student will achieve this. It may be appropriate with some students to discuss how they would welcome your support to help them achieve this goal.

9. Part amicably

A smile, appreciating their honesty and thought, wishing them a good weekend, indicating you are looking forward to teaching them again are just some of the small and significant ways you can add value to the process, repair and restore the relationship and positively influence the student's motivation for attempting to make it better next time.

Handling conflict

At various times, teachers encounter students who have become extremely angry and potentially physically aggressive. A natural response from the teacher will be to experience anxiety and even fear. If you combine these two states and remember the information given above, you can imagine that the chances of being 'emotionally hijacked' are high and therefore your chances of establishing a rational conversation are limited.

It is for precisely these reasons that we feel it is important for schools to have a clear mechanism in place to allow support to arrive quickly. While it is beyond the remit of this book to explore how this can be organised, there are some practical skills that can bring a degree of settling influence to these situations. It may be stating the obvious but the worst possible time to make decisions about how you should respond is when you are actually experiencing the situation. It makes sound sense, therefore, to have some clearly rehearsed strategies and language patterns available to you. Remember that the more choices of response you have, the calmer you can remain and the more influence you can exert.

In developing the following strategies for responding to anger, we thought it would be interesting (and quite fun) to explore the circumstances by which we could influence students to become angry in the first place. Here we offer some ideas that you may find helpful in many ways.

HOW TO CREATE CONFLICT!

✗ Put students on the spot	✗ Argue with students
✗ Shout loudly directly at them or about them	✗ Preach, lecture or blame
	✗ Create embarrassment
✗ Invade personal space	✗ Label them as their behaviour
✗ Move quickly towards someone	
	✗ Make personal or family comments
✗ Point or jab a finger in their direction	
	✗ Compare them unfavourably with peers
✗ Deny them the right of reply	
✗ Infer they are lying	✗ Shout them down
✗ Recall previous bad behaviour	✗ Think you must win
✗ Threaten sanctions	✗ Hold grudges

Clearly, sustaining any of the above strategies requires high levels of emotional arousal!

One of the most useful 'tools' for managing conflict is a positive working relationship with the student. Often referred to as an 'emotional bank account', the nature and quality of relationships are crucial factors when conflict occurs as they can significantly influence the intensity and duration of the conflict at worst and at best prevent it happening in the first place. Being *proactive* in building relationships (not friendships) with students is a vital preventative mechanism. Just like a genuine bank account, unless you have made regular deposits, you will not have an overdraft facility when you need it.

However, having some language-based tools to reduce emotional arousal and re-engage rationally with students is essential.

Some effective strategies

1. Agreement frames and validation

Establish rapport by gaining immediate agreement and validating (not necessarily agreeing with) how they may be feeling.

> *'I can see you're upset.'*
> *'I understand you have a point of view. When I have finished explaining this then I'll be able to listen to you.'*

2. 'I' statements

Describe events from your own perspective rather than the student's.

> *'When you shout out, I find it difficult to teach the others.'*

81

3. Check assumptions

Under stress we all say things we don't mean *literally*. Nevertheless, the words we use affect our emotional levels. Calmly checking meaning can reframe things into a 'softer' perspective.

> *'What you have said is physical threat to Lucy. Is that what you mean?'*

4. Emphasise choice and link to consequences

Help the student to take responsibility for the choices and resolve the situation.

> *'If you choose to walk out of the classroom now you will be choosing . . .'*
> *'If you hit Liam, who will be in the most bother?'*

5. Use double bind choices

Giving the impression of choice is powerful. Double binds are an illusion of choice and still have the same effect.

> *'I don't know whether you want to choose to cool off outside the room for a couple of minutes or if you want to just sit quietly here until we can discuss things calmly.'*

6. Make spatial decisions

Consider the differences between *intimate space (0–0.5m)*, *personal space (0.5–1m)* and *social distance (1–3m)*. Stay on the edge of personal space when things get heated but not so far away that your ability to relate and influence diminishes.

7. Consider other non-verbal skills

The use of a pause between responses reduces the adversarial nature of interactions. Equally, facial expression, arm and hand movement all need to convey non-aggressive intentions. Remember they are easily misinterpreted when you are aroused.

8. Remind student of strategies taught

If the student has received support for anger management, make yourself aware of any tips they have been taught. Ideally they would be contained in Individual Education Plans (IEPs), Individual Behaviour Plans (IBPs) or Pastoral Support Plans (PSPs).

9. Check out your scripts

It is important to be aware of the 'scripts' in your head during these times. Useful thought processes are:

> *'What does the student want from this?'*
> *'What is it I want from this?'*
> *'What's happening with my breathing, tone of voice, posture, etc.?'*
> *'Do I need to defer this until we are calm?'*
> *'Do I need assistance?'*

10. Use school-wide exit policies

Become familiar with the procedures of the school's exit policy. It is important to know how and from where you can get help quickly if needed.

11. Active listening

Keeping communication going is vital. Try to understand what the student is going through before you try to make yourself understood. Listening conveys respect, responds to feelings rather than actions and encourages the student to 'talk out' rather than 'act out'.

Slow head nodding, minimal encouragement (*'uh huh'*, *'go on'*, *'tell me more about that'*) and restating:

> *'You feel angry because you feel a detention isn't a fair sanction. What solutions do you have that allow me to teach and others to learn?'*

12. Focus on primary behaviours

At these times it's best to ignore the posturing and tones of voice that students may use and stay focused on the issue that is of concern.

13. Use inclusive language

When you linguistically connect two things that are seemingly opposed, it has the potential to create the possibility of a more useful response.

> *'It's OK to be angry and it's OK to sit quietly until we can talk.'*
> *'You can come with me and you can also have your say about this.'*

Questions for professional development

What do you feel about the topics covered in this chapter?

What are some of the implications of the topics within your classroom?

What do you think is the most important for you to remember from this chapter?

Maintaining a positive state

As we have stated in Chapter 2, a key belief is that self-esteem is a primary goal. We have explored the concept of self-esteem in much detail within *Creating Winning Classrooms*; however, we also felt it appropriate to offer some key ideas and thoughts to assist you in building strategies that support your own positive state. It is axiomatic to state that there is a strong connection between the ease of implementing (and remembering) all of the skills and strategies outlined here and in other books, which can comfortably be regarded as good practice, and our own feelings. Simply, when it looks like we are on top of things, when we experience a *sense* of well-being and when we feel positive about ourselves, we are far more effective. The fact is, effective practitioners deliberately and proactively engage in activities and hold on to thoughts and ideas that help them attain and then sustain a more positive state. After all, it makes sense that the first person on whom to exert positive influence should be yourself.

Obviously, it is beyond the scope of this book to explore all these ideas in detail; instead we offer the following as clues to your own approaches.

Refer to the idea of escalator language in Chapter 3 to ensure you include the temporal words in your explanations of what happens to you:

> '*So far* I haven't engaged this student enough *yet*.'
> '*Sometimes* lessons don't go the way I planned.'

Engage in appropriate self-talk

The idea of being able to get everything right when managing 30 plus different agendas simultaneously is, from a logical perspective, ludicrous. Making mistakes is an inherent part of learning. Indeed it is only by making them that progress is achieved. Refer to mistakes as 'feedback', 'results' or 'outcomes', as it normalises them.

Give yourself permission to make mistakes

Invest wisely	Make clear and deliberate choices about in whom you are prepared to invest your psychological well-being. Limit it to people whom you choose such as family and close friends. Dealing with a challenging child is never enjoyable and when it happens it doesn't take away, negate or erode the amazing qualities with which you enrich the world. The incident with the student is not part of your personality or identity. It is just something that happened and you will reflect on what (if anything) could be learned for any similar experiences in the future. Do not link your emotional well-being to your ability to manage troubled and troublesome students.
Organise your attention well	Whatever you concentrate on you will notice more. Focus the significant majority of your attention and consideration on the things that actually are going well. It is true, is it not, that most students are reasonably pleasant, follow instructions, speak to you in a fairly civil tone and are reasonably keen to learn? How much time do you spend thinking of the hugely positive influence you are having on their lives as you praise and reward them? Our guess would be – NOT ENOUGH!
Remember the zones of influence	Look back to Chapter 1 and the Zones of Influence and Concern. Someone once told us that there are only two things in life that you should never worry about. The first are the things you can do something about. The second are those things that you can do nothing about. When faced with dilemmas, always ask yourself, *'Which of these two applies here?'*
Take the blame	As you begin to notice more of the students who do well, learn and grow in your care, come to the frightening conclusion that it is extremely likely that it is your fault!
Take care of yourself	<ul><li>Sip water regularly throughout the day and cut back on tea and coffee.</li><li>Consider blood sugar levels and snack on fruit, sugary sweets, etc. during the day.</li><li>Take some time for you to eat. You are worth at least 20 minutes to yourself and your students are worth you taking the time for you.</li><li>Use music, either during or between lessons, that inspires and lifts you.</li><li>Place pictures around the class of things that capture your imagination – mountains, beaches, dolphins, etc.</li><li>Have pictures of your children, partners, dogs, etc. on your planner to remind you of how important you are and how you are loved.</li><li>Have access to fresh air. Open windows or walk outside as often as possible.</li></ul>

- Keep a Victory Log, noting all the things, however tiny, you achieve. Flick through it to remind yourself of the strengths and qualities you possess.
- Breathe deeply. Breathe out slowly for twice the duration that you breathe in. When you do this four or five times in a row you will become aware of your brain becoming quieter, your muscles softening and your heart rate slowing. It is an automatic bodily response. Obviously, you shouldn't maintain this pattern of breathing for long periods!

Appendix B

Some strategies

We felt it would be hugely appropriate to offer a readily accessible guide to some specific strategies that are proven not only to have a high probability of success, but are also totally compatible with all the principles outlined here and in *Confident Classroom Leadership* and *Creating Winning Classrooms*. Many of them have already been mentioned somewhere within the three books; however, this is the only place you will find them all together in one handy format. They are not in any particular order and merely offer you the chance to 'dip in' and try them.

The overall balance you achieve between catching them being good and catching them getting it wrong *is*, by most definitions, self-esteem. Be *proactive* and *deliberate* in noticing what students (and you) do that is acceptable and appropriate, not just the things that are exceptional. Telling the students what they are getting right *at the times when they are* offers a significant way of building self-esteem and helping them belong as well as significantly increasing the likelihood that they will repeat the behaviours.

Catch them being good

Decide what things can be ignored, how long for and importantly what you will do next if ignoring doesn't work. Some things should *never* be ignored – racist and sexist comments, unsafe or violent behaviour. Aim to *simultaneously* praise students for getting it right while ignoring others. There are two types of ignoring:

Planned ignoring

Simple: when you simply ignore what's going on and simultaneously acknowledge students doing the right thing, e.g. putting their hands up.
Prefaced: when you give a brief instruction before ignoring, e.g. *'when you're in your seat with your hand up then I'll help'* followed by turning away and ignoring.

Positive cueing Acknowledging or praising students for following instructions often encourages those who are off task and close by to follow suit. Remember to acknowledge them too as soon as you notice their success.

Proximity Moving to stand close to an off-task student or a 'chatty' table of students while continuing to explain ideas to the class can have an impact.

'Thanks' Finishing an instruction with the word 'thanks' rather than 'please' conveys a strong sense of expectation that they will do it.

The broken record approach Calmly repeating the direction two or three times without entering into any discussion can assertively reinforce your instructions. Accompanying this with an outstretched, open and 'blocking' flat hand (like a police officer stopping traffic) can help too.

Take-up time Take-up time or face-saving time is used in all interactions as a deliberate way of reducing the emotional heat. Simply give your instruction to a student in an assertive manner with appropriate eye contact, use 'thanks' and then lose eye contact by either scanning away to the rest of the class or by physically moving away to a different part of the class. Reclaim the agenda and maintain the momentum as you do this by engaging with another student who is behaving appropriately. This signifies that things have moved on and there is nothing more to add and crucially, it also gives students that brief amount of time to 'posture' by sighing or responding deliberately slowly – in other words save face with their peers.

Casual questions to refocus students *'How's it going here?'*
'Do you need a hand?'
'What's happening about the diagram?'
'Remember this needs to be finished by the end of class. Are you on target?'
'Can you think of another example?'
'Have I explained that well enough for you?'

Body language Appropriate body language is important. Some non-verbal behaviours will quickly trigger high emotional arousal as a pattern match. Recently a teacher described moving quickly towards a boy who instantly (and genuinely) cowered. This was clearly a disturbing example of a pattern match for the child. Keep movements fairly slow and avoid closing down personal space quickly or snatching work or other items without permission. Avoid also sudden loud noises. Use open hand gestures rather than finger jabbing and pointing. If in doubt consider what effect your body language would have on the most vulnerable member of your class. We have always found it useful to ask a trusted colleague to watch us and give us feedback on our non-verbal repertoire.

If you really want people to hear what you have to say, then it is important to validate how they may be feeling or thinking before they will hear you.

Validate and redirect

> *'You're out of your seat, Jack. What's up?'*
> *'I was just getting a pencil'* (whine, whinge).
> *'Yes, it's important to have the right equipment. Now back to your seat and carry on with the diagram. Thanks'* (followed by take-up time).

Rule statements or reminders

> *'Darren . . . (pause) . . . We've got a rule for asking questions and I expect you to use it. Thanks.'*
> *'Mike . . . (pause) . . . Disturbing others is against the rules . . . back to work quietly, thanks.'*

'When . . . then . . .'

> *'When you talk loudly then I can't teach.'*
> *'When you're in your seat then I'll check your work.'*
> *'When you've finished this task then I want you to be proud of yourself.'*
> *'When the lesson's over then I'll listen to your side of the story.'*

'What . . . ? What . . . ?' questions

There are three parts to the 'double what' skill. The first is an observational statement, *'I notice your book isn't open yet, Jenny.'* This then leads into the two questions, *'What are you doing?'* followed by (depending on the response to this), *'What should you be doing?'*

> Teacher: *'Aaron, you're out of your seat. What are you doing?'* (casual, conversational, pleasantly)
> Student: *'Nothing!'* (usually defensive and with a touch of strop)
> Teacher: *'What should you be doing?'*
> Student: *'I dunno.'*
> Teacher: *'You're supposed to be finishing your diary. Back to work now, thanks. I'll come and check it in a minute.'*

Sometimes students will argue back. The same skill can be applied.

> Teacher: *'Paul, Steve, (direct eye contact) what are you two doing?'*
> Student: *'Us?'* (surprise and indignation)
> Teacher: *'What are you doing?'*
> Student: *'Nuffink.'*
> Teacher: *'Actually you're talking loudly. What are you supposed to be doing?'*
> Student: *'Other people are talking too'* (defence and aggression).
> Teacher: *'I'm talking to you at the moment (calm but direct). What are you supposed to be doing?'*

Student: *'This project stuff'* (undisguised distaste and sarcasm).

Teacher: *'OK. I expect you to do your work. If you need my help let me know by putting your hand up. I'll come and check later'* (move off giving take-up time and expecting compliance).

NB. You may choose to talk to them after class about their attitude and response.

'I' statements

The use of the personal pronoun 'I' in a special way adds power and conviction to any direction.

Many of our messages have an unspoken 'you' at the start, e.g. (YOU) *'sit down'* or (YOU) *'for heaven's sake, shut up.'*

These messages usually blame and imply that the student in question has a problem. Notice how easy it is to shout when giving a 'you' message.

An 'I . . .' message acknowledges a problem and opens the way for a solution without blame and conflict. An 'I . . .' message contains three elements:

- The behaviour, e.g. shouting out
- The feeling, e.g. I get frustrated
- The effect, e.g. stopping me helping others.

'When you shout out, I get frustrated because it stops me helping Billy.'

Rule of three

Repeating the same direction more than two or three times to the same child on separate occasions for the same behaviour teaches them that you don't mean what you say and they don't have to take any notice. You may work some of the other strategies in between the repeated directions such as proximity, rule statements, etc. but there comes a point when you need to hold them accountable for their choices.

Consequential choice

This is a logical follow-up to the 'rule of three' approach and is characterised by an *'If . . . then . . .'* pattern of language.

'Sean, I've spoken to you twice about flicking bits of paper. If you choose to do that again, then you'll be choosing to stay back at break and clean up the classroom.'

Check your assumptions

Everybody makes assumptions; it's a natural thing to do. It only creates potential tension if you imagine that they are true without seeking more information. People often say or do things that they don't literally mean. By checking your assumptions out with students you are offering them a way out with dignity:

'Are you refusing to follow my instructions and sit here?'

'Do you realise you have threatened me? Is that what you meant to do?'

Between three and a maximum of five minutes away from the rest of the class (usually outside the room at secondary level) offering students the opportunity to reduce emotional arousal and consider things more rationally, reflecting on the potential consequences of their behaviour, is a sound and valuable strategy. A brief chat and firm restatement of expectation must preface return to class. Refer to 4Rs and previously good behaviour to support them back into the class.

Use time out

There will be occasions when students need to leave the class for the rest of the lesson as a result of not responding to a range of strategies and having moved through the sanctions hierarchy. It is vital that you understand clearly what these procedures are and how to operate them *before* you need to use them. We recommend discussing these within your department and referring to any school policies.

Use agreed school-wide exit procedures

References

Canfield, J. and Siccone, F. (1995) *101 Ways to Develop Student Self-Esteem and Responsibility.* Ontario: Longwood Professional Books.

Covey, S. R. (1992) *The 7 Habits of Highly Effective People.* London: Simon and Schuster.

DeBruyn, R. L. (1983) *Before You Can Discipline.* Manhattan, Kans.: The Master Teacher Inc.

Dreikurs, R. and Cassel, P. (1974) *Discipline Without Tears.* Manhattan, Kans.: Penguin Books USA.

Dreikurs, R. *et al.* (1998) *Maintaining Sanity in the Classroom.* New York: Accelerated Development.

Elton, Lord (1989) *Discipline in Schools.* Report of the Committee of Enquiry chaired by Lord Elton. London: HMSO.

Ginott, H. (1972) *Teacher and Child.* London: Macmillan.

Goleman, D. (1996) *Emotional Intelligence.* London: Bloomsbury Publishing.

Griffin, J. and Tyrell, I. (2000) *The APET Model.* Hailsham: The European Therapy Studies Institute.

Hook, P. and Vass, A. (2000a) *Confident Classroom Leadership.* London: David Fulton Publishers.

Hook, P. and Vass, A. (2000b) *Creating Winning Classrooms.* London: David Fulton Publishers.

Hughes, M. and Vass, A. (2001) *Strategies to Close the Learning Gap.* Stafford: Network Education Press.

Jensen, E. (1995) *Super Teaching.* California: Turning Point Publishing.

Mosak, H. (1999) *A Primer of Adlerian Psychology: The Analytic-Behavioural-Cognitive Psychology of Alfred Adler.* New York: Brunner/Mazel.

O'Donohue, J. (2000) *Eternal Echoes – Exploring Our Hunger to Belong.* London: Bantam Books.

O'Hanlon, B. and Beadle, S. (1996) *A Field Guide to Possibility Land.* London: BT Press.

Robbins, A. (1988) *Unlimited Power.* London: Simon and Schuster.

Rogers, W. (1994) *The Language of Discipline.* Plymouth: Northgate House.

The Royal Commission on Learning (1995) *For the Love of Learning: The Bégin-Caplan Report*. Ontario: Government of Ontario.

Wheldall, K. and Merrett, F. (1989) *Positive Teaching in the Secondary School*. London: Paul Chapman Publishing.

Lightning Source UK Ltd.
Milton Keynes UK
UKOW022102170512

192778UK00006B/1/A

9 781853 466922